I0488024

Profile of a Litigator

Profile of a Litigator

◆

(Personality Traits of the Personal Injury Attorney)

Patrick M. Ryan, J.D./Ph.D

iUniverse, Inc.

New York Lincoln Shanghai

Profile of a Litigator
(Personality Traits of the Personal Injury Attorney)

Copyright © 2005 by Patrick M. Ryan

All rights reserved. No part of this book may be used or reproduced by any means, graphic, electronic, or mechanical, including photocopying, recording, taping or by any information storage retrieval system without the written permission of the publisher except in the case of brief quotations embodied in critical articles and reviews.

iUniverse books may be ordered through booksellers or by contacting:

iUniverse
2021 Pine Lake Road, Suite 100
Lincoln, NE 68512
www.iuniverse.com
1-800-Authors (1-800-288-4677)

ISBN-13: 978-0-595-35534-1 (pbk)
ISBN-13: 978-0-595-80018-6 (ebk)
ISBN-10: 0-595-35534-X (pbk)
ISBN-10: 0-595-80018-1 (ebk)

Printed in the United States of America

Special Thanks and Acknowledgment to the Following Attorneys:

Peter C. Alessio
Alma R. Arlos
Valerie K. Aronoff
Craig F. Ashton
Robert M. Baskin
Earnest C.S. Bell
David J. Bills
Paul V. Bossenmier
Robert J. Brantner
Gary A. Case
Jim Joseph Childers
W. Stanley Cooke
James S. Crawford
Melvin L. Demoff
Michael L. Faber
Roy J. Fleischer, Sr.
Deirdre Frank
Robert J. Granucci
Thomas L. Hinkle
Andrew M. Hochberg
Gary Hursh
Kevin Hyatt
Richard I. Isacoff
Robert F. Jakubowicz
Melvin R. Keeter
Michael J. Kelly
David G. Knitter
John B. Lewis
Roy R. Levin
Donald G. McCallum

J. Douglas McGilvras
Michael L. Mierhead
Robert B. Mikel
Robert A. Montekone, Jr.
Timothy E. O'Laughlin
Archie G. Parker
William L. Plexico
Anthony J. Poidmore
Dawn M. Rich
Andres O. Rico
Frank L. Rowley
Lawrence M. Schulner
Dave Schultz
Jerry Scribner
Gloria Martinez-Senftner
John A. Sheehan
Richard S. Simmons
Edward A. Smith
Daniel J. Sullivan
Michael S. Van Sickle
Jack Vetter
James E. Vaughn
Howard J. Wasserman
Joe Weinberger
Danny G. Williams
Hollis R. Williams
William F. Wright

Contents

Introduction

You are in an accident and are injured. It was not your fault and you wish to be compensated for your pain and suffering. What to you do? The simple answer is that you do what millions of Americans do every year, you call a Personal Injury Attorney.

Then the question becomes, what is the personal attorney like, who is the personal injury attorney and how will the personal injury attorney act on your behalf?

These are some of the questions this book attempts to discuss in the hope that the common everyday person as well as the person contemplating a personal injury career can have answered for a better understanding into the insights of the personal injury attorney.

For the client or perspective client, you should be able to gain a better understanding of what the personal injury attorney does. When most people think of attorneys they think of the courtroom. However, most surveys show that lawyers spend more time interviewing clients than in any other professional activity. Additionally, included in interviewing clients is "counseling." The personal injury attorney spends far less time in court or in a library than he or she does interviewing, counseling, advising or making decisions with and/or for clients.

This book should not be considered the standard bearer of handbooks for the personality traits of a litigator. It can however be considered to be representative of the professional influences surrounding choices made in the law office. It can also be considered representative of a working definition of interpersonal communications between and among lawyers to clients and lawyers to lawyers.

To my knowledge no book before this work has dealt strictly with personality traits of the personal injury attorney and so this work will be the first full view of the subject. The instruments used herein, to gain a personality profile, are contemporary and valid for a study of this kind. While I may have borrowed from the instruments and the actual attorneys across the country responding to the instruments, I must bear total responsibility for how the ideas are interpreted and applied. While indebted to many, the blame is mine alone.

Special thanks to those who participated and whatever the detriments or benefits that may be derived from this book, I feel the profession itself will be better off for this beginning introspection of itself.

Cursory Profile

From the title of the book, we must assume that lawyers have personalities to have personality traits. Therefore, we will begin with holding this to be the case. We will learn from reading the text that litigation skills may stretch the spectrum from totally competitive to totally accommodating. However, whatever the strategy and/or tactic employed by the litigation attorney there is one personality trait that all successful litigators must have: CONFIDENCE. It is all right to be accommodating if the attorney is confident that this trait is appropriate in a given situation. Conversely, competitive tactics may be appropriate for alternative situations and some grouping in the middle of these two traits for other circumstances.

Self confidence is really a learned trait and in many cases one must earn confidence by first being on the losing end of an adversary situation. The good litigator can then turn the tables on his next opponent when in a similar situation the next time. Really, good litigators, when finding themselves faced with an opponent who speaks from a well spring of knowledge will simply boldly assert themselves in a plausible way. In other words, they at least give the appearance that they know what they are speaking about. If they still lose, so what!, they have learned for the next battle.

To be "in the game" as they say, the good litigator has to have an interest in the people and events that surround him or her. Taking an interest is important because unlike the garage mechanic, the litigator has many clients from different walks of life and can undertake cases that range from a rear end collision to brain surgery malpractice. Without an interest in various aspects of life, the litigator cannot do a professional job. Surely there are those in the personal injury field who specialize, but the trial lawyer must never rest and never cease to grow and improve.

The good litigator must be able to do more than just desk work and paper pushing. A necessary ingredient for the successful litigator is field work that may include investigations, meetings with experts, and of course the regular types of hearings either at court or in conference rooms or libraries.

While the successful litigator is a zealous advocate for his client's claims, compromise is an important aspect of success, both for the client and the attorney. Playing the zero sum game, winner take all, does not serve the client's best interests but more often than not, the client is the toughest person to convince of this. Knowing when to say when about going to trial is important but equally necessary is that a litigator feel comfortable about going to trial because it is the comfortable trial attorney who makes the best negotiator. Demands will not be met if it is felt by opposing counsel that you do not have what it takes to go to trial. This is important, as stated, but too simplistic as no good litigator wishes to go to trial where it is almost certain that economy will outweigh the integrity of a claim. A litigator who has confidence in going to trial will usually know when a compromise is in the client's best interest and not simply in his or her own interest.

Common sense and good judgment are two important personality traits of the personal injury attorney. This does not mean that common sense cannot also be intellectual or philosophical but however used, should be straightforward for the situation if influence is to be applied.

Finally, every successful litigator must maintain a sense of integrity. Reputations in the legal community circulate and one who compromises his or her standards will be at a loss. The merits of a matter may vary but integrity must be constant no matter who the client or what the costs and/or rewards.

Confidence relates directly to self-image and self-esteem. Litigators create their own reality with their thoughts, feelings and attitudes. The more lawyers' like themselves and see themselves as worthwhile and important, the more they appreciate and accept others and the more easily they can get along with others. This process really starts in the law school training ground arena. It is at this time that would be litigators learn to cope with other people's expectations, handle criticism and rejection, and overall, take charge of themselves. So whether the litigator is compromising, accommodating or competing, he or she, if successful, is secure within their own boundaries. The confidence they feel allows them to feel no need to prove anything to anybody.

Lawyers, as part of the petite bourgeoisie, do not need to depend on anyone other than the taxpayer for their means of production. This, in itself, allows the litigator some independence, ("have degree, will travel"). For the litigator, beginning in law school where they undertake a vocational/academic experience, they have comfort in the knowledge that their law school skills will transfer to a vital sense of worth, meaningful employment and positive perception from the general populace. I say that law school is somewhat vocational because the lawyer, while in school is acquiring tools to put in his or her tool box. Later on, when called to a job, the lawyer can apply the right tool to the job. Some litigators have been accused of walking around with only half a tool box!

This brings us to another aspect of confidence, which all good litigators must possess; competence. We have already mentioned self-worth and a sense of belonging through a sense of vitality, but every good litigator must also be able to deal with challenges and situations thrown at them. Normally, they must deal with new dilemmas and do so quickly while on their feet in the trial setting. Other tangible aspects such as self-worth and perceptions which turn to expectations on the part of others, and, again, in turn can become self fulfilling prophecies of success, are a neat and attractive appearance, intelligence, having to deal with pressure situations and money.

Most attorneys and especially trial litigators enjoy their work as it provides a sense of satisfaction to them. Therefore, success in terms of level and quality of living is icing on the cake. Most good litigators can expect to be savvy enough to maintain good health, have a good career without living meal to meal, create relationships of their choosing, not those thrust upon them as in the corporate world, have adequate recreation and leisure time and generally feel good about themselves.

All of the above comes from hard work, risk taking, initial debt, great sacrifice, strain on all of the feelings listed above and emotional and intellectual dissonance. But when the time comes, litigators restore their equilibrium and build upon what they have learned. Litigators, for the most part do not necessarily feel that they need to be "the best" for acceptance or approval. Oftentimes, others will say how lucky the attorney is while the attorney will respond that the harder he or she works, the luckier they tend to be. Litigators, although they do in fact posses confidence, must also take great pains to develop a sense of confidence in their clients. Clients come from various walks of life and range from the totally confident to the totally destroyed. Even those with confidence in their own circles of society will doubt themselves in the litigation arena. Therefore, the good litigator will give the client his attention, usually in the form of unconditional positive regard. The litigator, being sworn to zealously advocate even those causes that are unpopular, must never criticize or ridicule the client, they must listen attentively and show their acceptance of the client dilemma.

High self-esteem and confidence makes all the difference in the world to the litigator. The litigator has worked hard, followed his or her dream, knows that there will be failures, takes responsibility, and feels good about him or herself because he or she does take charge of their destiny and needs and more often than not, they do so with the appreciation and admiration of others.

Being a litigator is not an easy job to get but most who do aspire and succeed really like their work. They get attention and have their needs of safety, security, respect, esteem and self actualization met.

Lawyers are in fact equipped to give legal advice. Most lawyers, after the passage of time, become more well rounded. Their knowledge base expands with each different case handled.

It is a widely held belief that lawyers breed litigation. However, please be alert, while reading this book, as to whether or not our litigators' avoid useless conflict or create it for increased income.

Background of Topic

The idea behind this work came to me while completing my initial courses for my doctoral degree. (This work represents my dissertation for a Doctor of Philosophy in Education Degree.) The importance of understanding, communicating interpersonally and collaborating are vital to the personal injury attorney. In fact, most attorneys decided to go into the profession to have a sense of vitality and enrichment in their lives within their respective communities. Vitality must be transactional, not unilateral.

To measure attorney personality traits, 375 questionnaires were mailed to attorneys on both the east and west coasts. The initial questionnaires were 25 pages in length and contained approximately 75 questions. After having received 3 returns by the proposed deadline, it became apparent that streamlining the questionnaire was in order. A second mailing went out which consisted of one sheet of paper, double sided, and contained approximately 55 questions, mostly true or false, to the same 375 attorneys. The questionnaire was broken into four sections that included "Self Monitoring," "Rhetorical Sensitivity", "Machavellian Scale" and a "Conflict Mode Instrument".

Of the 375 questionnaires that were mailed to attorneys in California and Massachusetts, approximately 300 were to defense oriented personal injury firms. Surprisingly enough, or maybe now I should say not surprising at all, approximately 70 plaintiff attorneys returned the questionnaires and only 1 defense firm returned its questionnaire. The one returnee was a junior associate who has been practicing for approximately 2 years. Obviously each attorney's speculation as to the interpretation of the returns will vary somewhat, but my particular interpretation, in a nutshell is that the billing syndrome precluded participation. Additional reasons why attorneys act or do not act will be woven in throughout the fabric of this text.

Therefore, as you can see, this book primarily concerns itself with the plaintiff personal injury attorney. Of the approximately 70 attorneys who did respond, ages varied from 29 to 72. The average age was 49, the middle age was 43 and the most common age was 46. The law schools of the responding attorneys are listed in the acknowledgment at the beginning of this book. Of the 70 responding attorneys, approximately 62 were men and 8 were woman. The number of years in practice varied from 2 to 63. The average was approximately 10 years, the middle number of years in practice was approximately 15 and the most common number of years in practice listed was 12.

There actually were a few more than 70 who answered but, for the most part, 70 answers per question were given as a few either could not decide on an answer or inadvertently skipped questions.

Because our lawyers are over the ten year learning curve, I submit that they like what they are doing and will continue to practice law. Also, because most are plaintiff attorneys I would submit that 90% of our litigators are also solo practitioners, who run their own businesses. This says to me that they are more accessible to the average citizen. It also tells me that they have more than business acumen. They obviously generate good will and growth through increased demand. To have achieved this situation, these lawyers must have provided reassurance and guidance to many clients along the way. This means that they must be somewhat personable.

Purpose and Importance of the Study

The prevailing notion that we have become a "litigious society" is no illusion. The simple fact of the matter is that almost anyone will sue anyone else at the drop of a hat. Most middle class America now fears that obtaining the American Dream of owning a home can also work against them as an open invitation to be sued. Additionally, with more and better communications we have all heard of the plaintiff who "got $1 Million Dollars even though the police report said the accident was his fault." This then is the mentality that the lower class or unemployed person is laboring under. I say lower class or unemployed because most of this litigant mentality bombardment comes in the form of television commercials which run during the day while most people are at work. Additionally, in recent years, systematic access to medical treatment without insurance or prior payment has become available to the person who is injured and has grounds for a lawsuit. In effect, there is really no good reason why someone should not sue and more often than not the "I've got nothing to loose" mentality prevails. This mentality can also work to the plaintiffs detriment as he or she is less inclined to put "good money" in their pocket, thinking instead that a "spin of the wheel" will yield more.

Therefore, this book should have something of interest for everyone, including a plaintiff, past, present and future, a defendant, past, present and future, as well as attorneys and the health care system. Knowing why attorneys act the way they do will be of great benefit to the above listed persons.

Power, control, influence and how these items are gained or lost through the different roles the personal injury attorney plays is the essence of this work. Performing effectively in different exchanges necessarily requires behavioral relationships tied to situational events. This book will attempt to analyze creativity, mechanical proficiency and humanistic skills. We will see how language and communication helps the attorney control power and exert influence. Behavior will vary with the roles they assume. How open we are with ourselves, each other and situational timing all requires appropriate behavioral responses and summons us to use memory, experience, and learned characteristics of what we consider to be acceptable.

No study of this kind can take place without having made certain assumptions, (hypotheses), ahead of time. For the non attorney reader, these assumptions may include ideas that the personal injury attorney will do anything at anytime to anyone all for the sake of winning. Other closely held beliefs may include that the personal injury attorney is perceived as devious, manipulating and uncaring. Other terms that may come to mind are forceful, competitive and immoral. Terms that often are not associated with the personal injury attorney include problem solving, sharing, accommodating, smoothing and avoidance. After having read this book you will be able to see which assumptions prevailed and which failed.

Although this work is based on 70 attorneys' answers, I will submit to you, the reader, that whether 70 or 7000 attorneys answered these questionnaires, the results would not vary significantly. However, I think there would exist very slight differences if one were to test only attorneys in the northeast, only Hispanic attorneys, only female attorneys, etc., etc., etc.. In sum, then, the importance and purpose of this study is to dispel or affirm such prevailing and closely held beliefs. I believe, in this era of "lawyer bashing", that the reader will gain interesting insights into the personality traits of the personal injury attorney. For those whose beliefs are affirmed, you may well have learned the why behind the actions of a litigator and for those whose beliefs are dispelled, you may want to reflect on why you held your past beliefs. Needless to say, anyone who works closely with the litigator will not be as surprised at the results as the person, for instance, a client, would be, as a one time piece of a litigation puzzle.

F. Lee Bailey has been quoted as saying "the public regards lawyers with great distrust. They think lawyers are smarter than the average guy, but use their intelligence deviously. Well, they're wrong. Usually they're not smarter".

This statement tells me that lawyers aren't devious. It also tells me that intellectual ability is not the key ingredient in the legal field. Where a page of history is worth a volume of logic, rules and procedures, when mixed with facts and persuasion, are more important than just being plain and honest if justice is to prevail.

Statutory rules must exist to protect the plain and honest but it is also the same rules that confuse the average guy. For instance, no one can go into court without John Doe and still be able to say what John Doe knows. What if John Doe does not want to come to court because he can't get away from work or because he will be out of town during trial. The simple answers are that you either subpoena or depose John Doe. Unfortunately, these are things the plain and honest average guy doesn't know how or when to do.

Testing Instruments

This work, entitled Profile of a Litigator, Personality Traits of the Personal Injury Attorney utilized four separate testing instruments. They include a Self-Monitoring Scale, a Rhetorical Sensitivity Scale, a Machavellian Scale and the Conflict Mode Instrument.

The Self-Monitoring Scale distinguishes high self monitoring individuals from low self monitoring individuals. The source of this scale is from the "The Many Me's of the Self-Monitor, by Mark Snyder and his article was contained in *Psychology Today*, 13 (March 1980): 34. Reprinted by permission of Brooks/Cole Publishing Company: Pacific Grove, California.

Studies indicate that high self-monitors (1) demonstrate more social skills, (2) can communicate a wider range of emotions, (3) learn faster how to communicate in new situations, (4) show more self-control, and (5) seem more friendly and less anxious than low self-monitors (Lippa 541-59).

The next test instrument used was the Rhetorical Sensitivity Scale by Roderick R. Hart and William F. Eadie from their work entitled "Attitudes Toward Communication and the Assessment of Rhetorical Sensitivity", printed in *Communication Monographs*, 47 (March 1980): 6-7.

The Rhetorical Sensitivity Scale measures such things as sensitivity, honesty, accuracy, distortion and supportive climates, and is used with permission of the author, Dr. Eadie.

The third test instrument used is the Machiavellian Scale designed by Richard Christie and Florence L. Geis in their book on Social Psychology entitled "Studies in Machiavellianism" published by *Academic Press* in 1970.

The "Machiavellian" is someone who views and manipulates others for his or her own purpose. The scale measures participation or lack thereof in interpersonal relationships, concern or lack thereof of conventional morality, how one views others and levels of ideological commitment.

The fourth and final test instrument used is entitled the "Thomas-Kilman Conflict Mode Instrument" by Kenneth W. Thomas and Ralph H. Kilman, by *Xicom, Incorporated* which is a copyright and is being reproduced by permission.

The Thomas-Kilman Conflict Mode Instrument is designed to assess an individual's behavior in conflict situations. The range of behaviors are from assertiveness to cooperativeness, each to the extent that an individual attempts to satisfy his or her own concerns.

Each testing instrument will be elaborated upon under its appropriate heading.

Like most things that are learned, lawyers have repeated their behaviors before they "owned" then.

No one can absorb knowledge fully having only encountered it once or twice. After about five times it will become sensible and easier to deal with. The same is true for the contents of this book. You may want to read it all in one sitting or by bits and pieces. This is why each testing instrument has been contained in its own chapter.

The academic reader will notice lack of standard statistical methodologies and this is due in large measure to the fact that each testing instrument has its own scoring method.

Please feel free to browse, to turn back and forth and to repeat for maximum understanding.

Questions to Be Answered

Some of the more popular notions concerning litigators to be answered through this study include:

1. All lawyers care about is winning.

2. All lawyers care about is money.

3. All lawyers care about is power.

4. All lawyers are basically immoral.

5. Lawyers will do anything for money.

6. All lawyers will lie to win.

7. All lawyers are sue happy; and

8. All lawyers are egotistical and self-centered.

The existence of these notions, if held by clients, can and does affect client/attorney decisions. This fact is very important in and of itself because, to the client, feelings are facts. This being the case, clients can oftentimes appear and/or act defensively toward the attorney and the legal situation when they sanctify feelings and thereby elevate form over substance.

At the conclusion of this work, we will be in a better position to evaluate whether or not the above notions are justified.

There are no statistical standards of error or deviation and no null hypothesis. This is a one-shot case study which does not, in this work, expose the test group to a re-test. There are multiple comparisons and multi-treatment inferences with carry-over effects from one test to another. There is also observer bias even though I try to be objective. The answers are the product of naturalistic observation and I, as the observer, do not control or manipulate the responses as given. The sampling was random and taken from the Yellow Pages from Northern and Southern California and Western Massachusetts.

A hypothesis is a tentative, reasonable and testable explanation for the occurrence of certain behaviors and events. The degree to which these tests measure what they have intended to measure, or their validity, is commensurate with the objective individual scoring.

1

The Process

Before explaining the results of our litigator profile it is important that you first have somewhat of an understanding of the personal injury litigation structure. Even though some would espouse that attorneys are profiteers just waiting in line to make money from your injuries, please consider that you wouldn't do surgery on yourself and you really shouldn't go through the litigation process alone either. Although you may feel you alone are the best person to know your claim, i.e., how the accident happened, you should know that if you are without an attorney, this information alone will not be enough to settle or win your claim. You must remember that just because a person slips and falls or is hit by another car, that person is far from being automatically entitled to a recovery. Liability and damages must be proven. Litigators are in the best position to know how to structure your claim. As a Mandatory Continuing Legal Education lecturer on personal injury I will provide a brief synopsis of the personal injury litigation system in linear progression.

The process really starts when a person is injured and feels that someone other than himself or herself was the cause of the injury. Normally, most people in the personal injury litigation process are initially without a past or present attorney and therefore turn to advertisements to select an attorney.

Most litigation candidates will normally select an attorney with experience, free consultation and someone who works on a "no award, no fee" basis. Having done this, the initial consultation takes place where the client and attorney will sign a retainer agreement. Normally, fees for an automobile accident are thirty-three and one-third percent and fees for a slip and fall accident are forty percent. The reason for the higher fee for slip and falls is that normally some kind of an investigative work up is necessary and therefore the attorney knows going into the claim that it will provide him with some monetary exposure, normally around $300 to $500 just to find out if you have a valid claim. Where there is an automobile accident there is usually a police report generated which provides a ready made investigation of the facts and sometimes of liability as well. Also, at the time of the initial consultation, the client will need to sign additional forms such as a medical authorization so that the attorney may request medical records and bills to prove the damages issue of the claim and, depending on jurisdiction, other forms may be necessary. If the claimant is employed at the time of the accident then a wage loss form is given to the client to bring to his or her employer for completion.

After the initial consultation the attorney will customarily send a letter of representation to the person or entity responsible for the client's injury. This letter will request that the person or entity make his or her insurance company aware of the pending claim so that the insurance people also have an opportunity to investigate the facts, circumstances and possible damages of the claim. Most importantly, you do not want to sue someone without coverage because, more often than not, the resulting resolution of the case is without a monetary recovery.

Because liability or fault is the most important component of any claim, (without proving fault even a million dollar medical claim is worthless), at this point the attorney will try to "pin down" the liability issue by retaining the services of investigators and experts. Statements must be taken and preserved, photographs also preserve evidence, measurements, clothing, appliances and engineering aspects such as accident reconstruction based on skid marks or anti-slip coefficients of friction must be obtained.

The client and attorney must work together as a team to prepare and present a claim for damages honestly, fearlessly and thoroughly. Therefore, it is vital that mutual trust, confidence and complete cooperation exist which means that a full disclosure of all information is necessary up front to avoid future surprises.

Many claims can be settled informally and out of court without the necessity of formally showing proof of liability or damages. Naturally, most cases of clear liability, one way or the other, will settle before trial. For a case of good/strong liability, most persons or entities with insurance coverage will pay on a claim to avoid future costs of litigation, as a hedge against a "runaway verdict" and to avoid any future goodwill or litigation problems with their own client. In the case of a bad/weak liability case, the plaintiff attorney will normally disclose to the client that the claim's integrity is outweighed by the economy of following through on such a claim and will therefore normally attempt to terminate the claim in the most beneficial manner before the exorbitant costs and expenses of a trial.

Before an insurance company even sends a claim file to an attorney or law firm, an adjuster will try to informally resolve the matter by taking a recorded statement of the claimant and witnesses and by gathering all pertinent medical records and bills which arose as a direct result of the accident. At this phase of the pre-litigation process, the claimant's attorney and insurance adjuster work together to arrive at a resolution. Obviously this exchange cannot take place, in nine out of ten cases, before the claimant has completed his or her medical treatment. This is because no claim can have a true value without completion of underlying medical treatment and damages. The amount and extent of special, out of pocket expenses/damages, provides a reasonable basis for determining the amount of general, pain and suffering, compensation. Additionally, most states will apportion damages based on comparative fault. In other words, if a claimant has $1000 in medical expenses and is awarded an additional $5000 in general damages but is 50% at fault, then the total award would be $3000 rather than the original $6000.

It is when the claimant and respondent cannot agree on ideas of liability or value that a lawsuit will be filed so that eventually, after more of an investigative work up, a neutral trier of fact or even a jury can render an opinion as to the strengths, weaknesses and value of the claim. Additionally, in cases of serious bodily injury or death, it is normally standard that a lawsuit be filed so that the person being sued may be represented and have the benefit of full legal representation before paying large sums of money.

The filing of a lawsuit officially begins the litigation process. During the interval between the filing of a lawsuit and a trial there usually are depositions, interrogatories and independent medical examinations. Also, most jurisdictions schedule arbitration and a settlement conference in a maximum effort to settle the case before trial.

Depositions normally take place in an office conference room setting with both attorneys and the claimant present, during which time opposing counsel will ask questions about the accident and injuries of the claimant, all of which are taken down by a court reporter.

Also during the progress of litigation the other side may request that the claimant be examined by a physician of their selection. Under the law, they are entitled to such an examination. Before this process and before the deposition process takes place the claimant's attorney will arrange to prepare the client for these events. Ethical preparation by the attorney and client can help secure settlement. Even though the examination is called an independent medical examination, it hardly ever is because the doctor is normally a tool of the insurance carrier. Going through such a process without a trained litigator in your corner is not recommended. Most litigants without an attorney tend to exaggerate their pain and scream bloody murder when touched by the hands of the physician. Client's need to be reminded not to be afraid, to pay attention and to be candid.

In addition to depositions and independent medical examinations, each attorney may submit written questions called interrogatories for the other person to answer in writing. These answers, like the deposition procedure are given under oath and penalty of perjury. Any subsequent substantive differences in answers at trial and the opposing attorney has the right to read, to a trier of fact, the prior answers for purposes of impeaching the claimant's testimonial and character credibility.

Trials are traumatic experiences and the major benefit the litigator provides is to obtain a fair and just recovery for the injuries and damages a client has suffered as a result of an accident. Most lawsuits are settled before going to trial. However, the litigator must always be prepared and willing to go to trial in each case if that is necessary to obtain a just and adequate recovery. If an insurance company believes the litigator is trial shy, a proper settlement will not be offered. Effective negotiation requires that the litigator have faith and confidence in the merits of the case and the evidentiary work up to stand firmly for what is right.

Arbitration provides the first glimpse at the strengths and weaknesses of a claim and does so in a low cost manner. Trials themselves are expensive because of jury fees, court reporter costs, and expert witness fees. Normally experts are necessary to be successful at trial and sometimes are necessary just to get evidence in before a jury under rules of evidence. For instance, a treating physician's diagnosis, prognosis and opinions are vital and yet the treating physician may charge from $350 an hour to $6000 for a half day of testimony. Therefore, the benefits of an arbitration, with somewhat relaxed rules of evidence, is obviously in the claimant's interest because ultimately the claimant must bear the brunt of trial expenses. The litigator customarily fronts the costs but costs are recoverable from an award. This is why in many cases a client can accept a sum lesser than the full potential of the claim and still put more money into his or her pocket. Insurance companies are well aware of this fact and have the wherewithal to take advantage of this economic exposure consideration. For instance, if a true arbitration award of $10,000 is rendered, the defense will reject it and offer less knowing the plaintiff will have trial costs. In other words, if the plaintiff receives a verdict of $10,000 at trial, $2000 will come off the top for costs.

Arbitrations are where the dispute is referred to an impartial third party, normally agreed upon by each side, to hear the merits of the case and render a decision. The arbitrator will try to render what he or she believes a jury would render. The benefit of this process is that attendance of experts is usually not necessary and that, unless the parties agree otherwise, the arbitration is non binding and can be rejected, whereupon further litigation ensues.

Most cases settle at or shortly after an arbitration at what is called a settlement conference, which is the client's last opportunity to settle before a formal trial.

As you will see throughout the remainder of this work, the litigator is not only an advocate but a counselor as well. Therefore the litigator must maintain a strong, workable relationship with the client so that the mutual interests of each may best be served. The number one way to build and maintain good client relations is "communication". However, as you will see throughout the remainder of this work, communication can be a strange animal.

The following points are some areas that concern communication which clients do not like, and, as you will discern, litigators must oftentimes walk a fine line. Clients do not like lawyers who do not keep them informed. Clients do not like lawyers who do not return their telephone calls or lawyers who talk and write in legalese. Clients do not like lawyers who do not answer their questions or who pontificate rather than explain. Clients do not like lawyers who are too timid but also do not like lawyers who are too aggressive. Clients do not like lawyers who have no confidence in their own ability and worth or lawyers who do not seem to get around to working on their case. Clients do not like lawyers who appear insensitive to their concerns or who make promises they don't keep. Finally, clients do not like lawyers who treat the client as an adversary, seem to care about nothing but fees and who are blunt and tactless about dashing the client's hopes.

Conversely, the attorney must watch for client danger signs which include but are not limited to the client with more than one previous attorney, a client with a self righteous or irresponsible attitude, the client who gets advice from a friend or relative, the client who wants the litigator to handle the case from the sidelines, the crusading client who wants to litigate for a principle, the client who is non responsive to advice or questions, changes the subject a lot, does not listen, and repeats the same questions. Additionally, clients who complain about trivia, fail to keep appointments and talk about lawyer incompetence in order to get the lawyer to cut his or her fee is a clear danger sign.

It should be explained to the client that the only reason to sue is to obtain money and if they are suing for any other reason then the litigation process is the wrong place because money is all the litigation process can award to make a person whole again.

The presentation of a case is both a science and an art. The litigator's adherence to an application of rules, procedure and practice constitute the science. The litigator's adaption of strategies, tactics and techniques constitute the art.

Advances in technology are constantly changing the way litigators prepare to try cases, but in the end, effective presentation of a case by a trial lawyer will be the product of many factors including experience, preparation, devotion to the client's case, an understanding of professional ethics and an internal standard of excellence.

Common examples of concerns for a plaintiff in a personal injury case includes the payment of an obligation, the value of human life and the importance of public safety.

Please keep in mind while reading this book that I have tried my best to give useful and accurate information. Naturally the results contained herein are and will be subject to differing interpretations and you are certainly free to come to your own conclusions. Nothing contained herein is guaranteed about a litigator but I do hope it serves a purpose in presenting general facts and attitudes which you, the reader, can take with you the next time you find it necessary to work with a lawyer.

The responses to the test instruments should provide a measure of potential to predict how the litigator is likely to perform in a future situation. The instruments and population group provide an in-depth investigation of individuals within the legal profession. The tests determine the factors and relationship among factors which have resulted in the current behavior or status of this case study.

The statistical significance here is that the results occurred by chance and not control and are therefore the real thing. Distribution levels are not extreme or skewed scores and responses are representative of the profession as they exist in equal proportion. Although the instruments are not completely unobstructed, (they could not fill in their own answers), participants were free to choose among a range of responses.

2

Self Monitoring Scale

The first instrument used was the Self-Monitoring Scale which distinguishes high self monitoring individuals from low self monitoring individuals. The source of this scale is from "The Many Me's of the Self-Monitor, by Mark Snyder in his article contained in *Psychology Today*, 13 (March 1980): 34. Reprinted by permission of Brooks/Cole Publishing Company; Pacific Grove, California.

Studies indicate that high-self monitors, (1) demonstrate more social skills, (2) can communicate a wider range of emotions, (3) learn faster how to communicate in new situations, (4) show more self-control, and (5) seem more friendly and less anxious than low self-monitors (Lippa 541-59).

This test measures whether a "true self exists which is apart from the social roles we play. Supposedly, high self-monitors are aware of the impressions they are making and are constantly looking for ways to fine tune their performances.

The concept of the self has been around since the beginnings of human nature. It is psychological in nature and is always measured within the yardstick of other persons perception of self. It really is no longer a simple matter to flatly state that people are consistent and stable; that is to say that honest people are always honest or that generous people are always generous. Those who are liberal today can be conservative in the next year. Just as litigators have an identity, this identity can take the form of many selves. Because the identity or self one brings to bear on a situation changes with the vagaries of the circumstances, self personality traits will also vary. A good example of this is the trail setting. F. Lee Bailey's cross examination of Mark Fuhrman during the O. J. Simpson trail varied greatly from his other examinations. In effect, Mr. Bailey became a different personality dependent upon the personality he encountered and the task at hand. Different personalities have long been a trademark of the litigator. It has often been said that the "cross-examination" is the "great engine of truth" and if this is so then the litigator is the person putting the "petal to the metal" as it were.

Listed below, and for further discussion is the Self-Monitor Scale with the results of the survey contained therein. <u>Self Monitoring</u>

I find it hard to imitate the behavior of others.
(44)   (30)

I guess I put on a show to impress or entertain people.
(32)   (40)

I would probably make a good actor.
(42)   (29)

I sometimes appear to others to be experiencing deeper emotions than I actually am.
(23)   (49)

In a group of people I am rarely the center of attention.
(26)   (45)

In different situations with different people, I often act like very different persons.
(35)   (38)

I can only argue for ideas I already believe.
(23)   (46)

In order to get along and be liked, I tend to be what people expect me to be rather than anything else.
(13)   (59)

I may deceive people by being friendly when I really dislike them.
(39)   (34)

I am not always the person I appear to be.
(40)   (31)

Totals (317)   (391)

As you can see, on the face of things the scores appear to be fairly evenly distributed. The proper scoring method is to receive one point for each of the questions 1, 5 and 7 that were answered with a false and one additional point for each reaming question which was answered with a true. Except for question number one which preponderantly favors true over false, questions five and seven were answered false over true by almost a 2 to 1 margin. Additionally, questions three, nine and ten were answered true in the majority. Question three scored by almost a 2 to 1 margin while questions nine and ten barely scored true over false. Overall, from the approximately 70 answers received, a score of six was obtained. Please do not worry at this point about the statistical analysis.

The test scoring indicates that this group of litigators are not high self monitors. A score of seven or above means that you are a high self monitor and a score of 3 or below indicates low self monitoring. Obviously then these litigators lean toward being high self monitors but are not overly concerned with their impression management skills. However, they clearly are somewhat aware of the impression they give to others because they scored far from being low self monitors.

The self monitoring scale measures how concerned people are with the impression they are making on others, as well as building to control and modify their behavior to fit a particular situation. This monitoring of self is a personality trait that is different from other normal personality traits such as the traits which will be measured later on in this work.

To be a high self monitor, one need not possess an overabundance of intelligence or belong to any particular socioeconomic status. Additionally, high self monitors need not necessarily be an extrovert, overly anxious or have a strong need for acceptance. For the most part, high self monitors may be somewhat power oriented or Machiavellian, however, as you will see, these individuals do not necessarily score high on the Machiavellian Scale. The Self Monitor Scale has proven to be valid and reliable.

People who are sensitive to the ways they express and present themselves at social situations are most likely to be the ones who choose to create and maintain an appearance, with or without a specific purpose in mind. This high self monitoring type of person will pay careful attention to the way others respond to their appearance, assimilate signals and cues and then develop a new "fit" by adjusting their performance to have a desired affect.

Low self monitors, on the other hand, are not as concerned with an appearance as much as they are with being able to express how they feel and what they think rather than mold and/or tailor their behavior to please or lead others.

Obviously there are advantages to being able to monitor and adjust ones behavior, the most important of which is to get what one wants. Some people and classes or groups of society are better at the self monitoring game than others. Salespeople almost exclusively rely on self monitoring to gain their desired results.

In fact, it is entirely possible to over exaggerate these signals and responses. We probably have all been in the situation where a sales ploy was overly obvious and became extremely aware that the salesperson would say or do almost anything to get the sale. Politicians, actors and litigators are also included in the most likely groups to be high self monitors. Naturally, more than mere words are necessary for successfully communicating your awareness of understanding and fitting a situation and mannerisms can be equally effective as a form or representation. In effect, these groups of people are performing to exercise control over their respective environments. Notwithstanding the above interpretation of high self monitors, to be able to effectuate this kind of performance it is essential to be able to control one's motions. In the courtroom, for instance, while under the close scrutiny of the jury, a litigator must constantly be aware that any emotional reaction can almost certainly be interpreted as a testimonial response. A good example of this is the plaintiff attorney who takes great pains to rehearse with the plaintiff the testimony to be given while on the witness stand only to find that while on the stand, the plaintiff is coming out with unanticipated or unexpected answers. If the attorney appears agitated, frustrated or starts leading the witness for the desired effect, then normally the opposite effect will be presented. Therefore, the litigator, as a somewhat high self monitor must be adept at detecting impression management of self and others. They must intentionally and/or purposefully be expressing themselves accurately both verbally and facially. The performance becomes polished with experience where the personal injury litigator is aware of the personality trait he or she is using.

A score of 6 for attorneys should not seem all that unlikely. Unlike salespersons or actors who play the part, attorneys oftentimes are the part, in other words, they shape, form, lead and persuade what perceptions could or should be.

Obviously, from the test results given above, many attorneys are high self-monitors. These are the kinds of litigators who seek out cues and constantly attempt to "read" patterns in an effort to understand others. This kind of trait in the personal injury litigator is not only commendable but worthwhile given that hundreds of thousands of dollars that are spent each and every year in an effort to determine how jurors will react in any given situation. Most high self-monitors tend to conform to and become part of a situation, displaying the behavior most appropriate for audience benefit. On the other hand, low self-monitors are, for the most part, unaffected by discrepancies in apparent perspective differences. For this type of litigator, their own personal attitudes and dispositions are believed to be an accurate enough representation of the reality they perceive.

Although litigators, appear to be high self-monitors more often than not, this does not necessarily mean that they use their impression management skills for deceptive or manipulative purposes. Rather, more often than not, these types of skills are used to promote smooth social and/or client interactions. Generally speaking, motives of high self-monitors are difficult to measure. However, where situations tend to repeat themselves a number of times, motivation is more readily apparent. In other words, for the litigator, where a page of history is worth a volume of logic, the structured and familiar settings a litigator deals within tends to make motivation predictable. During these regular settings, the litigator can overcome shyness and take a more active and controlling role in interpersonal discourse. In fact, given the regularity of situations for litigators, most newcomers to the process, (clients), expect and even have a need for the high self-monitor litigator to take charge, to lead through control of conversation and generally be the more directive member of the pair. In sum, it is the litigator who must manage, create, encourage and maintain a smooth flow of behavior for both him or herself and the client and/or trier of fact, be it a judge, arbitrator or jury.

Given the above characteristics it is not difficult to imagine that the high self-monitor normally emerges as a leader. Given also the results of our litigators' answers to the survey, where most participants have already passed a ten year learning curve, they have become adept at knowing when to take the bull by the horns and when to just plainly take bull. In either event they never really feel they have relinquished management, but have the instincts to know when they can influence a situation directly and when a situation needs indirect placement.

Taking a closer look at the survey results we can see that for question number one, "I find it hard to imitate the behavior of others" the majority of the answers were "true", 59.5% to 40.5%. Simply put this tells us that lawyers do not nor are they really expected to imitate the behaviors of others. This comes as no surprise as the litigator is usually in a position of superiority and center of attention where he or she controls and shapes rather than imitates. The plaintiff litigator, the person who must synthesize the trial really stands in a position of authority. He or she possesses the information and expertise that other participants do not. Therefore the litigator has formal authority to direct activities of others and personal powers of persuasion to accomplish a specific purpose. However, they must still be attentive and responsive to their witnesses character and jury cues.

The second question on the self-monitoring scale, "I guess I put on a show to impress or entertain people" was answered false in the majority by a 55.5% to 44.5% margin.

I will suggest to you here that almost all participants in this study are plaintiff attorneys and that a more exaggerated finding would probably show if the study was completed by a majority of defense attorneys. The fact that only one of three hundred one defense attorneys answered the survey is indicative of this. However, the above result to question number two, suggests that for the most part, litigators are competent and make positive efforts to create trust between the people surrounding them. Trust having been established it becomes safe to express ideas and feelings freely and to take risks. This is the stock in trade of good communications and, as mentioned in the beginning of the book, where attorneys help to create self-esteem and confidence in clients, they can ask for honest feedback when they work. Additionally, the litigator is a listener and can take the posture of being the learner in many situations which increases productivity and success in terms of litigation and monetary results. In short, rather than putting on a show, the majority of litigators would rather collaborate for maximum results. This, however, is not to say that some showmanship does not take place in the courtroom where showmanship is more of a teaching methodology than just trying to impress or massage an ego. In the end, ego's will always give way to fact management when it comes to jury verdicts.

Question number three of the survey states, "I would probable make a good actor". 59.2% answered affirmatively. Does this mean the other 40.8% should take acting classes or just that they have confidence as the "Columbo" type. I don't know the answer to that question but I can surmise that skill recognition can sometimes walk a fine line between myth and reality. When it comes to interpreting perceptions like these we are really betting on the instincts of the individual who answered one way or the other. In other words, necessity is the starting point of what the task demands when the litigator goes to trial. Each litigators' understanding of their own abilities, contributions and needs in order to win will vary greatly. Perhaps then some attorneys believe that because they are able to adequately balance what must be done and what would happen if certain behaviors were not communicated either verbally or non verbally to a jury that they feel a great sense of fulfillment through a trail experience. Litigators also feel these traits can be matched and transferred to other areas, such as acting. On the other hand, the simple explanation is that lawyers, especially trial lawyers are often portrayed on television and in the movies and most true trial attorneys believe they can do as well if not better, which makes them think they can be good actors. They are optimistic in assessing their talent.

Regardless of the above, it may in fact became necessary for attorneys to become actors if the O.J. Simpson trial is any indication of modern trends. I will have more to say on allowing cameras into the courtroom toward the end of the book. I am for and support continued and increased use of cameras in court-rooms.

High self-monitors are able to see beyond the masks of deception. This goes hand in hand with gestures in the courtroom, if we are to be successful in under-standing intentions we must have the ability to be in tune to the cues which take place.

Statement number four relates "I sometimes appear to others to be experienc-ing deeper emotions than I actually am". Again, approximately 68% of the attor-neys elicited answered "true" while 32% said, in effect, "what you see is what you get". I believe a proper interpretation of these results reveals that the majority of those answering are high self-monitors. Low self monitors tend to accept behav-ior at face. Without seeming contradictory, high self monitors avoid prejudicing situations with their own attitudes and behavior and in fact will mask their true attitude because this, to some extent is what they have been trained to do. For instance, they have an ethical responsibility to support positions that are unpopu-lar for their clients. Interestingly enough however, high self-monitoring individu-als prefer low self-monitors as people they prefer to be around. This is because high self-monitors prefer a stable and predictable social environment and there-fore seek consistency from those displaying accurate and true feelings and emo-tions.

The strong minority showing of low self-monitors in our group of attorneys will be attracted more to the agreeable person even though that person may attempt to ingratiate himself to the monitor for obvious motivational purposes. In bare bones form, I believe the reason for such a high showing on this question is because most attorneys pictured themselves in conversation with clients and/or in negotiations with opposing counsel on behalf of their clients when answering. In order to be successful, as stated earlier, attorneys need to control the emotions they are experiencing in order to achieve their goals.

The response received to statement number five may come as a surprise to all non-lawyers. The statement reads as follows: "In a group of people I am rarely the center of attention". 63.3% seemed to think they are the center of attention while 36.7% believe they are not most of the time the center of attention or at least, more than rarely the center of attention.

The reasons for this response may range from personal perceptions of perspec-tive on the part of attorneys to a more conscious maintaining of physical distance between themselves and others. Both reasons have validity in our present "temper of the times" regarding attorneys. Attorney bashing is not uncommon and therefore it is not unreasonable for attorneys to avoid those who may be unfavorable to them individually or as a profession. Another conscious perspective may be that attorneys distance themselves so that they will not have to assume the role of accessible adviser. They find that others will often seek legal consultation or opinions in social settings.

Statement number six reads "in different situations with different people, I often act like different persons". This was a close call for the attorneys which made up the random sampling of our population group, with 52.7% answering "false" and 48.3% answering "true". Here, the message is clear in that most people are quite flexible in their self presentations and are persuaded to become the person that most wins the approval and favor of those around us. The clear message given by our attorneys to this question disregards notions of seeking favor and approval. Rather, the would be actor in a law office does not transgress the boundaries of his or her true role because by exceeding the role of true self, poor working relationships and poor professional results are produced. The idea is that respect for the competence of one another is better based on respect for one's own competency than on a theory of roles and the limitations of roles. The litigator favors truth and although he or she may be somewhat concerned about being accepted and liked, the professional has more concern with order, articulation and accuracy. The lawyer realizes that if he or she is only responsive instead of accurate, then he or she may find themselves in a trap. When lawyers become overly concerned about whether or not what they say will sound good then when the time comes to truly respond they may find they cannot fulfill a true professional role because they really haven't listened.

Idea number seven states that "I can only argue for ideas I already believe". It should be no surprise that the majority answered "false" by a 66.6% to 33.3% margin. I say this is no surprise because litigators are under a duty to be zealous advocates for their clients, within the bounds of the law. For the most part this means that the lawyer must give his or her client their unconditional positive regard. Actually, what is somewhat surprising is that almost half the attorneys surveyed said they will not argue for ideas they do not already believe. Keeping in mind that most of the attorneys responding to this survey are, (1) personal injury attorneys and (2) seasoned veterans, it is not unplausible to assume that these attorneys are now somewhat in a position to "pick and choose" clients and causes. First of all, most plaintiff personal injury attorneys did not just start off practicing personal injury law. Most attorneys start their careers by practicing every field of law that puts food on their table, including criminal, family, probate, landlord/

tenant and contract. After building a monetary reserve, they then begin a personal injury practice. Therefore, it is not unreasonable to assume that for the personal injury attorney who started out taking any and all injury cases he or she could, would thereafter try to improve their situation by spending their time only on the cases whose integrity will outweigh wasted economy.

Aside from the Code of Professional Responsibility, common sense must always prevail when deciding to undertake a borderline matter. A litigator should bring to bear his or her experience and objective sense to the decision making process to understand whether or not a cause is morally just and/or legally permissible. Obvious modern examples include a client claim which is illegal but seems moral and the opposite, the conduct which is legal but seems immoral. These kinds of decisions are more for the criminal law advocate whereas the civil litigator is more or less faced with choices that ask if client behavior serves the public interest, i.e., frivolous or fraudulent claims, harassment claims and self serving claims. The dilemma for the civil litigator is to recognize or know where the public interest lies. To this end, he or she must make value choices that are subjective and hold him or herself in ultimate accountability when the voices of public discontent arise. In other words, the lawyer, once choosing to accept a cause must assure client freedom and pursue goals which may seem to be contrary to public interest. However, as all students of history realize, popularity, decorum, and propriety in the public interest changes over time. In fact, if not for zealous advocates, much of our present a public interest would not presently be in place. Modern technology dictates that the personal injury attorney constantly discover new truths concerning birth rights, product liability and emotional health.

Consistent with the above analysis, statement number eight of our survey relates, "In order to get along and be liked, I tend to be what people expect me to be rather than anything else". Approximately 82% of those survey answered "false" while only 18% answered "true". Here the litigator is a low self-monitor, choosing instead to create a climate of openness rather than having environmental positions imposed upon them. Self determination is obviously then somewhat important to the litigator. Having ideals threatened by others, although sometimes very subtle, the legal counselor and advocate requires a resolute effort to achieve self awareness even in the face of negative reactions. High self-monitors have many selves and although the litigator may appear shrewd and pragmatic to fit conditions just as the high self-monitor would, the litigator is more single minded in purpose and regard their actions as consistent and stable. Inherent in and critically important to a proper understanding of why litigators overwhelmingly said they do not and will not act just to please others is because they deal from a position of authority. This certainly is not to say that they have some kind of raw power but rather that they understand the importance of being prepared and take responsibility. Being prepared helps the litigator deal with pressure situations and high stake situations that require his or her leadership. Being prepared creates an overall understanding of a situation that allows attorneys to monitor behavior and check for compliance of others rather than self. Being prepared helps the litigator be fair and act for just cause rather than have to resort to arbitrary or unreasonable assertions.

Statement number nine reads, "I may deceive people by being friendly when I really dislike them." Again, this was a close call for the attorneys who responded. The results are almost even for both true and false. By a slim majority there were more who responded true than false. The actual results were 53.4% true and 46.6% false. These results seem to indicate that half of the group strives to meet client requirements and to continually improve the way they do it while half continue to pursue their goals in an individual executive manner. The difficulty in interpreting these results is not knowing what position the respondent saw him or herself in when responding. Did the litigator answer based on interpersonal communications with clients, jurors, judges, opposing counsel or just regular everyday social contacts. My interpretation, being a plaintiff personal injury attorney, is that they considered clients first, jurors second and opposing counsel third. The plaintiff personal injury attorney is, for the most part, a sole practitioner. Therefore the litigator of this type is a manager of his or her own business and a supplier of services. Unlike the modern day defense firm which has a bureaucratic organization where decisions are made on the basis of position, tradition or the experience of the top management, the plaintiff litigator must manage by fact. This means that the plaintiff litigator is the only person to know what the solid data of his or her organization is and does not act on someone else's hunches. The results of this survey, given the population pool, suggests that the litigator places a strong value on truth, the way he or she sees it and learns from mistakes of approach, attitude, planning and human assessment for future success. Half have found that best results emanate from truth while half have found that a more calculating approach yields better compliance.

Finally, question number ten states "I am not always the person I appear to be." 56.3% answered "true" while 43.7% answered "false." To illustrate this point consider the following:

As the authors state in their article, "consider the case of a woman on trial for a crime that she did not commit. Her task on the witness stand is to carefully present herself so that everything she does and says communicates to the jurors clearly and unambiguously her true innocence, so that they will vote for her acquittal. Chances are good, however, that members of the jury are somewhat skeptical of the defendant's claims of innocence. After all, they might reason to themselves, the district attorney would not have brought this case to trial were the state's case against her not a convincing one.

The defendant must carefully manage her verbal and nonverbal behaviors so as to ensure that even a skeptical jury forms a true impression of her innocence. In particular, she must avoid the pitfalls of an image that suggests that "she doth protest her innocence too much and therefore must be guilty". To the extent that our defendant skillfully practices the art of impression management, she will succeed in presenting herself to the jurors as the honest person that she truly is (Snyder 40).

It often can take as much work to present a truthful image as to present a deceptive one. In fact, in this case, just being honest may not be enough when facing skeptical jurors who may bend over backwards to interpret any and all of the defendant's behavior, nervousness, for example, as a sign of guilt".

Through use of this illustration, it becomes apparent that the successful litigator, whether dealing with a client, associate, superior or jury must use behavioral skills to show others that they care. By behaving in a manner that shows you care, the litigator increases accuracy in use of words and gestures which can share what they feel and think. This increases others ability to perceive and understand in accordance with the litigators pre arranged priorities and according to the immediate needs of the client. There is no right or wrong way to do this, every litigator, over time, develops his or her own personal style. But one thing is important for the plaintiff personal injury attorney who has invested his or her own time, money, effort and work into a case file, he or she quickly learns that presenting an attitude which is uncaring quickly translates into bankruptcy. Each of us generally uses a variety of different behaviors for any given situation. Personal proclivities and predispositions can assist in judging how appropriate conduct can assist in realizing goals only if they are truly involved in what they are saying. The successful litigator has no difficulty separating himself from the person he or she is trying to understand and advocate for. Litigators must be low self monitors for attorney-client stability when with clients and high self monitors when presenting client claims to others. Equally true however, it is just this kind of understanding that the good litigator uses to finish a case file even before its ultimate conclusion. The litigator must be honest enough to know when he or she has done their best and can no longer represent the best interests of the client in terms of calculated returns.

The litigation profession has many characteristics and behaviors that are difficult to change. In this profession other people seek out our advice because they have problems and concerns which are both professional and personal. While the litigator should be a good listener and give unconditional acceptance to clients, the litigator must be careful to avoid getting so personally involved in another's situation that it seriously interferes with their own goals, needs, responsibilities and the time available to meet them. In other words, no matter how hard the client pushes, the litigator must understand that he or she is still running a business and did not go to law school and take risks or go into business to lose money. The bottom line must still be that attorneys must make the most effective use of their strengths and minimize potential weaknesses that reduce economic, esteem, decision-making and problem-solving effectiveness.

Litigators are not overly high or low self-monitoring people. They strive to keep communication meaningful and continue to utilize the most effective method for a situation. Lawyers are students of communication both verbally and non verbally. The most important aspect the litigator can lend to a continuing practice to improve skills is to recognize them during implementation. When putting on a trial the litigator is really only able to bet on the instincts of the juror pool. However, by speaking with jurors and clients, attorneys can receive evaluation on behaviors for proper future interaction. There are no rules or strategies per se, adapting communication behaviors depends on the litigators' understanding of principles they learn from past experience to match and transfer communication to meet the needs of the task and relationship at hand.

3

Rhetorical Sensitivity Scale

This chapter will concern itself with the second of four test instruments and will focus on the Rhetorical Sensitivity Scale. By way of introduction, the Rhetorical Sensitivity Scale is a testing instrument that measures various ways of thinking about what should be said and then deciding a way to say it. There are no right or wrong ways to approach interpersonal communications which will be measured by this testing instrument, rather the instrument will allow us to determine whether our litigators are "noble selves", "rhetorical reflectors" or rhetorically sensitive". Additionally, the test hopes to communicate such things as sensitivity versus rigidity, concern for self, concern for others and tolerance for situational thinking. Some of the questions contained in the test instrument are "dummy" questions which have no importance and are not including in any test result measurements.

The original Rhetorical Sensitivity Scale contained 40 questions, was administered to over 3,000 college undergraduates from sixteen highly diverse institutions and has test/retest validity and reliability. In essence, the rhetorical sensitivity measurement has its importance and usefulness in our complex society where interpersonal exchanges based on a rhetorical perspective can help people cope pragmatically with a range of human associations.

The authors describe the rhetorically sensitive person as an individual who willingly characterizes himself or herself as "an undulating, fluctuating entity, always unsure, always guessing, and continually weighing potential communicative decisions" (Hart 1).

By way of further background, "noble selves believe in being honest and forthright in expressing their ideas and their feelings. They are not very much concerned about how others will react to their frankness. At the same time, it is probable that they anticipate that others will be as open as they are. The responses of listeners do not influence noble selves in shaping their messages.

Their communication is linear rather than transactional in that they prepare and send a message and appear unaffected by any response thereto.

Reflectors, on the other hand, lack a concept of self or have an extremely low self concept. Because they are not sure who they are, they are both anxious and insecure. Their responses simply mirror the attitudes and behaviors of the other person. Reflectors are passive people who seek the approval of others. At first blush you may think reflectors as high self monitors because they can mirror situations. However, this is obviously not the case.

If we put noble selves at one end of a continuum and reflectors at the other end, the middle ground would be the "sensitive person". Sensitive persons are high self monitors who avoid the rudeness of noble selves and the timidly of reflectors by communicating tactfully to other people. Being tactful means saying what is appropriate in a given situation that will not offend the other person (Mader 239-40).

The questions and responses to the Rhetorical Sensitivity Scale are as follows:

<u>Rhetorical Sensitivity Scale</u>

A = Almost always true   C = Sometimes true   B = Frequently true   D = Infrequently true   E = Almost never true

A   B   C   D   E

People should be frank and spontaneous in conversation.
(A=15)   (B=35)   (C=20)   (D= 1)   (E=0)

An idea can be communicated in many different ways.
(A=55)   (B= 16)   (C=2)   (D=0)   (E=0)

When talking with someone with whom you disagree, you should feel obligated to state your opinion.
(A=2)   (B=ll)   (C=40)   (D=17)   (E=0)

A person should laugh at an unfunny joke just to please the joketeller.
(A= 1)   (B=8)   (C=32)   (D=20)   (E=12)

It's good to follow the rule: before blowing your top at someone, sleep on the problem.
(A=30)   (B=31)   (C=7)   (D=3)   (E=0)

When talking to others, you should drop all of your defenses.
(A=1)   (B=4)   (C=21)   (D=21)   (E=27)

It's best to hide one's true feelings in order to avoid hurting others.
(A=2)   (B=10)   (C=45)   (D=10)   (E=3)

No matter how hard you try, you just can't make friends with everyone.
(A=30)   (B=21)   (C=10)   (D=6)   (E=4)

One should keep quiet rather than say something that will alienate others.
(A=4)   (B=25)   (C=34)   (D=9)   (E= 1)

You should share your joys with your closest friend.
(A=40)   (B=27)   (C=6)   (D=0)   (E=0)

These ten questions represent the first ten of forty questions that appeared on the original questionnaire. Questions numbered 2, 6, 8 and 10 are all "dummy" questions.

The scoring key is as follows: for the Rhetorical Sensitive scale, C = 2, B or D = 1, A or E = 0. For the Noble Selves scale A = 2, B = 1, all others = 0. For the Rhetorical Reflector scale, E = 2, D = 1, all others = 0. Additionally, for proper scoring it is necessary to reverse the direction of certain items before scoring. I will not go into the entire methodology in the text but rather will refer the interested reader to the actual article as listed earlier in this work under the title Testing Instruments.

The first two responses need no reversal of method. The first statement reads: "People should be frank and spontaneous in conversation." On the Rhetorical Sensitive scale our litigators scored a 76, the Noble Selves scored a 65 and the Rhetorical Reflectors scored 1.

It should be noted that these statements do not necessarily measure interpersonal competence but rather is a mind set which some persons find useful in their everyday lives. Five constituent parts of the overall scale attitude are; (1) Acceptance of Personal Complexity where role takers realize their is no single real self; (2) Avoidance of Communicative Rigidity which calls for interpersonal and inventional flexibility; (3) Interaction Consciousness which is the heart of the matter and contrasts the rhetorically sensitive attitude to the Machiavellian attitude, (where one's own ideas and feelings are sacrificed to placate others), and the unconscionable egoism, (which sends messages without regard to the needs of others); (4) Appreciation of the Communicability of Ideas where the rhetorically sensitive person realizes that even proper ideas should sometimes not be communicated; and (5) Tolerance for Inventional Searching where rhetorically sensitive people realize that there is more than one way to skin a cat (Hart 2).

Therefore, for our group of litigators the rhetorically reflective person is virtually non existent. The rhetorical sensitive and the noble self appear to be almost equal when responding to the first statement. This is not all that surprising because attorneys often find themselves placed in different climates, i.e., generally they are in supportive climates with clients and a more defensive climate with opposing counsel. In any event it would appear that our litigators have adopted a middle ground for a workable agenda that includes not only openness but self awareness as well. Supportive climates offer more disclosure while defensive climates reduce the efficiency of interpersonal communications. However, for the attorney, as the expert, oftentimes it is necessary to forsake a true dialogue based on experiential insight of choices. The attorney/litigator as a professional person may be just as likely to change communication patterns to please others as they are firm in their predictive techniques. It would seem that for purposes of interpreting this statement that the litigators are being situationally expressive. The results of the first statement seem to clearly indicate that the attorney is not necessarily self centered or socially determined. Rather there seems to be room for some interaction consciousness between peacemaker and fighter.

Statement number two reads: "When talking to someone with whom you disagree, you should feel obligated to state your opinion". The rhetorical sensitive response received a total of 108 points, the noble selves scored 15 points and the rhetorical reflectors scored 25 points. It seems clear that the middle ground rhetorically sensitive person is by far the most favored approach by our litigators. It also appears that both the noble self and the rhetorical reflector are traps which, on a continuum, are either inclinations to boast which lowers another's self concept and esteem or is an inclination to avoid which may defeat the purpose of self and the other. Feedback is a two way street and the idea behind feedback is to help guide behavior for effective attainment of goals. To achieve this somewhat sensitive subtle style, lawyers sometimes need to be non judgmental and temperate when communicating. There is an old saying in the law that "even dogs know the difference between being tripped over and being kicked". The difference is an attitude which, in situational interactions, reinforce one's tendencies that underlie climate. In other words, our litigators are not quick to pass judgment but rather find that adapting a behavior and an attitude that is undomineering presents offerings for individual and collaborative choices. It is also apparent from the responses received that the attorney is aware that a force of character or force of own terms may be an exercise in futility. Generally such behavior shows a lack of respect that is perceived and reacted to negatively which, in turn, leads to disagreement, independence and shuts down the flow of information. In essence it is a no win situation.

In a 1960 survey of attitudes toward lawyers it was discovered that lawyers tended to think of service factors such as results, honesty and efficiency to please clients while clients regarded friendliness as the most important factor of client satisfaction. Therefore our litigators are correct in taking the middle road of the rhetorical sensitive approach instead of a sharp, formalistic, scientific approach for the legal health of their professional relationships.

Statement number three reads: "A person should laugh at an unfunny joke just to please the joketeller." Again, the rhetorical sensitive approach scored highest with 92 points, second was the rhetorical reflector approach with 44 points and the noble self scored 10 points.

The results of this statement point out a common scheme which is that most litigators do give time and attention to dealing with the human aspects of their relationships. Very few of our answering attorneys seemed insensitive to the joketeller and while a good number of our respondents would choose to reflect the other's behavior, this discourse is of questionable relevance, responsibility or real objective truth value.

However, the importance of being rhetorically sensitive and/or a rhetorical reflector can be found in avoidance posturing which gives the impression that you do not consider yourself to be more important. Our litigators understand that "going along" in this case adds expression, reduces hostility and cultivates personal rhythm which elicits gratefulness and capitalizes on good will. This result is useful in understanding that although the general population has a low opinion of lawyers, most people who consult lawyers have a higher opinion of the lawyer they do consult. Both form and substance have a place in problem solving and perception evaluation. One value of the more pluralistic rhetorical sensitivity approach is that it enables the attorney to resolve unnecessary disputes and conflicts that arise simply from a divergence of concepts. The deepest significance of such an approach lies in the fact that it is basically open ended and necessitates future interpersonal communications. Thus it is no accident that given successful rhetorical interaction that negative emotional and substantive involvement can be reduced. Proper rhetorical structures contribute to a larger dialectic purpose between understanding of reality and the aesthetic fascination of process between attorney and client. Rhetorical sensitivity wets the psychological aspect of a professional relationship to the whole of things for a truer and more concrete representation of effort. Because the litigator sees attitudes and motives as the primary content of communication, his or her attitude in understanding the nature and resources of rhetoric helps him or her to interact more effectively for the purpose of producing a together kind of response. Such rhetorical development verifies and acknowledges the paradox between personalities and issues which must be dealt with in direct proportion to the degree to which they are situationally individualized. In other words, the personal injury litigator goes through a litany of events that the client has little familiarity with and through exploiting rhetorical resources, the attorney exerts persuasion for the primary means of effecting client identification toward the process and the hierarchy of evolutions within that process. The art of rhetorical sensitivity begins understanding and involvement without overreaching or canceling it.

In a nutshell, rhetorical sensitivity is the art of communication.

Statement number four reads: "It's good to follow the rule: before blowing your top at someone, sleep on the problem." Our respondents answered scoring 48 points for the rhetorical sensitive approach, 91 points for the noble self and 3 points for the rhetorical reflectors. Here the respondents are saying, in quite unwavering terms that it is best to sleep on the problem. This statement called for a reverse of direction. Half of those surveyed took a middle ground approach while only three persons said flatly that they would not delay giving someone a piece of their mind. I believe these results show that the litigator is more of a communicator, collaborator and contributor than a challenger. It also shows that professional relationships are held in higher regard than personal freedom. The responses demonstrate an encouragement over discouragement approach and suggests that taking a hard view towards this kind of situation, no matter how justified, can be heavy handed and destroy a supportive and positive climate. Given that our respondents are plaintiff attorneys and not associated, for the most part, with a large firm, these results tend to indicate that their source of power is developed by him or herself and not provide by any organization. Our attorneys power base is grounded in information, expertise and good will which influences a commitment effect rather than a compliance or resistance effect that authority and discipline elicits. Additionally, the fact that most of our population group is older and professional is a clear reason why sensitive attitudes prevail. For the most part attorneys are not really in a supervisory position and their relative success depends on establishing and maintaining effective human associations. Naturally, there is a time and place for positional changes but I believe that given that most of our respondents have already experienced a median 10 year learning curve, their experience has taught them that effective leadership is based more on personal powers of persuasion than raw authority.

The fifth statement of the Rhetorical Sensitivity Scale reads: "It's best to hide one's true feelings in order to avoid hurting others".

In this day and age where "everyone is a critic" it is good to know that, our litigators, being representative of the profession as a whole, responded overwhelmingly that it is indeed best to avoid hurting others. The rhetorical sensitive approach scored 110 points, the noble selves only 14 points and the rhetorical reflectors scored 16 points. Basically, what this says is that the reflectors would almost always avoid hurting others, the noble selves would rather be true to their beliefs and to "let the chips fall where they may" while the rhetorical sensitive attorneys would size up the situation and necessity and/or lack thereof before speaking.

The litigators who did respond realize that two heads are better than one. For true collaboration to exist, those collaborating must do so voluntarily and have, at least for the task at hand, a coequal status. Therefore, any domineering approach will destroy mutual trust and debilitate interest and attitude. In most situations the lawyer must not lose sight that the personal needs of the client are facts and therefore a litigators' personality may, in fact, determine the results at hand. Some lawyers are fighters and relationships break down, some are peace makers and relationships get away from them. Each risk encountered by choices of behavior is hedged by self awareness. Our group of lawyers seem to have determined a point between the extremes of openness and deception that allows them to induce appropriate changes. Accurate self insight and constructive feedback are essential for effective bargaining to occur. Naturally, every litigator shifts roles over time and by being aware of our different roles and their effects, we lessen doubt on our interpretations.

The final statement on the scale reads: "One should keep quiet rather than say something that will alienate others. Again, the rhetorical sensitive approach was most favored by the respondents, scoring 102 points while the noble selves scored 33 and the rhetorical reflectors scored 20 points respectively.

As psychologist Solomon Asch stated, "the noble individual is robbed of human integrity by the insidious pressure of the group". Our rhetorically sensitive litigators are not really deprived of anything by acknowledging that conflict resolution is person philosophy prominent. Clarifying issues and setting expectations through mutual understanding is not only expedient but dignified. Lawyers live in and effect changes in systems and through proper decision making approaches can manifest themselves in humanistic fashion. Creativity will exist as long as people harbor a hope and optimization that things can be better in their lives. The main objective for the litigator is to serve the interests of his or her client. To this end, competition may be inevitable but conflict is not necessary.

I recently got "on line" and started to "surf the net." One of the first things I did was to hook up with the legal talk available on the net. I mentioned that I was writing this book in response to messages already on the net. One response I received from another attorney went like this; "so what have you found out about personal injury lawyers personality? Without the benefit of doctoral research to back me up, they seem to be lone wolves for the most part interested in David v. Goliath types of fights that occasionally pay well."

It would seem that this attorney has "bought into" popular conventional wisdom. His connection is so intimate, in fact, that until most attorneys actually confront these philosophical issues through such expressive techniques as these testing instruments that substantive interpretation and manifestation of true "self will give way to an archetype agency of personification. The universality of the legal system and its players engaging in a manner perceived by many to be negative is a myth perpetuated by the occasional and unusual but noteworthy contempt for the "deep pocket" or "runaway verdict" case. However, what most do not universally perceive is that the unusual but newsworthy case is all but a fragment of an otherwise true form of operation. Unfortunately the true nature and discovery of the litigation picture has become caught up in the relations of news production and class conflict rather than the dynamics of historical development and modern engagement. In sum, most of us only hear of, and therefore think of the worst which is misleading just as any part of a whole story. I believe this psychological profile should help, or at least begin to relay a distinction between what is perceived and what is functional.

Finally, you know, now that I think of it, there are probably a lot of litigators out there, including our respondents who like to think of themselves as the lone wolf or the hired gun, but, when it comes to action, well, you see the responses! Maybe its a kind of illusion that helps them behave and handle work pressures with drive and/or an enlivening enjoyment. I know I sometimes say things like this to family and friends, but rarely would I ever entertain those thoughts while on the clock as it were.

As a side note, please understand that all statistical analysis is mine alone and no comparisons were made with any standardized base groupings. Therefore, so far, our group is moderate to high in impression management, (self-monitors), but with enough flexibility to shape and mold opinion as well as react to it, they are rhetorically sensitive, that is, middle ground, knowing when to say when and when not to say when, unlike those who would always be skewed one way or the other.

4

Machiavellian Scale

The third test instrument used in our study is the Machiavellian Scale. Surprisingly enough, for reasons I could say I really don't understand, but I guess I do, most people would naturally associate Machiavellian tendencies with litigators. Traditionally the Machiavellian person was thought of as someone who views and manipulates others for his or her own purposes. For our purpose we will be concerned not with any historical concepts but as a source of ideas about those who manipulate others.

General characteristics of the Machiavellian type of person are: (1) a relative lack of affect in interpersonal relationships; (2) a lack of concern with conventional morality; (3) a person who errors in evaluating individuals and situations, thereby distorting perceptions; and (4) low ideological commitment.

The Machiavellian Scale used in this work contains six questions, four of which measure tactics and two that measure views. Questions one, two, three and six measure tactics while questions four and five measure views. The testing instrument with results is as follows;

Machiavellian Scale

The best way to handle people is to tell them what they want to hear.
(T= 10)   (F=65)

One should take action only when sure it is morally right.
(1X39)   (F=31)

Anyone who completely trusts anyone else is asking for trouble.
(T=34)   (F=38)

The biggest difference between most criminals and other people is that the criminals are stupid to get caught.
(T= 6)   (F = 68)

It is hard to get ahead without cutting corners here and there.
(T=15)   (F=56)

When you ask someone to do something for you, it is best to give the real reasons for wanting it rather than giving reasons which carry more weight.
(T=54)   (F=16)

People who are self absorbed will attempt to establish that they are superior. These people will always feel justified in making judgments because they are always right. When you talk to people like this you may get the impression that you are being manipulated by them for their own selfish needs. Manipulators believe that if they employ the proper strategies, they can get anyone else to do just about anything they wish them to do. Manipulation can take various forms, such as monopolizing conversations, talking loud, ridiculing others, appear to be impatient, stare in disbelief, avoid eye contact or seem shocked, insulted or hurt. If all else fails they may use silence. Manipulators score high on the Machiavellian Scale and therefore would be called high Machs. You have already had an opportunity to view the scale and can probably already determine the level of Machiavellian views and tactics of our population group. High self monitors, although somewhat power oriented are not necessarily manipulative. As you know, so far in our study, our sample population group is pretty much a moderate bunch and for the most part have displayed open mindedness. Open minded people generally encourage discussion and cooperation in problem solving arenas. Additionally, litigators are, for the most part, spontaneous persons and spontaneity usually gives rise to good will expressions.

This paragraph contains a digression from the present topic. Our study has its shortcomings, and I'm sure you will be able to think of many others that I don't list here, but remember, this study does not differentiate between males and females, socioeconomic levels, religious beliefs, political affiliations, correlations with other tests or any of the above and there was no retest or attempt to discriminate interpretations any more than what you find herein. While background material may be brought to fore in future works, please remember that, with the budget and organization used for this work, it was difficult enough to elicit the responses I was fortunate enough to receive.

The first Machiavellian statement is a statement of tactics and reads as follows: "The best way to handle people is to tell them what they want to hear". Sixty-five out of seventy-five answered "false."

It is possible that true manipulators are so clever that they fake low on the scale but this is really very highly unlikely. This statement has to do with honesty and represents a forced choice format. The respondents in our group, for this statement, must be considered low Machs. To simplify interpretation, and because this test was given to a group and not an individual, it would appear that most litigators strongly disagree that it is necessary to act unethically to get their way. This is a situation where litigators are dealing with others and must take into consideration such factors as maturity, satisfaction in present achievement level, cooperation and a pro social philosophy. Our litigators were less concerned with any measure of effectiveness that comes with manipulating others than they were with influencing by knowledge the pattern of others. The implications of the statement go deeper than what appears on the face of it. To have answered "true" implicates a form of gamemanship, by concealing information from another it tends to, in the long run, be viewed by other Machiavellian results, to create new situations which will be more stressful for them and for those who were honest to start with. Normally, whether internally or externally, those that create a lie also create skepticism, malabsorption, misfortune, malfunctions and future resistance by implication. Therefore, for this statement we can say that low Machs are more ethical than high Machs. This statement should not indicate any extremes such as absolute falsehood versus complete truthfulness, and although 10 litigators chose to handle people differently than the majority of the group, we should be mindful that the behavior of the high and low scorers may be more truthfully considered in terms of ability to influence anothers' attempts than in terms of adherence to abstract ethical beliefs. Although this test instrument is void of face to face contact, the present research was undertaken to compare high and low Machs among attorneys for purposes of interpersonal and/or offensive manipulation and the legitimacy thereof. Present day attorneys are oftentimes viewed as being manipulative and lacking in ethical or moral behavior. At the risk of alienating our group from attorneys as a whole, I believe these statements represent common situations in which deception may be viewed as legitimate. It seems reasonable, also, to assume that most people practicing special skills are skillful at interpersonal manipulation and may even find it congenial. Additionally, for those people not practicing special skills, the present day mind set seems to indicate that these people expect persons, such as litigators, to think up and perform more unsuggested and innovative manipulations. However, at least as far as statement number one is concerned our litigators appear to be ethical and moral. Keep in mind however that our group is educated and experienced and know social limits of situational tactics. Perhaps in a situation that requires cooperation from others they know how to test and stretch the limits without breaking them. After all, we know that our group is rhetorically sensitive.

The second statement on the Machiavellian Scale reads: "One should take action only when sure it is morally right". Our group was closely divided on answering this statement, with 39 answering "true", 31 answering "false". This statement may, in fact, be somewhat ambiguous and in ambiguous situations high Machs tend to regard power positions as appropriate while low Machs tend to compromise. High Machs are opportunistic under ambiguous conditions and low Machs seek public approval and objective evidence to validate their positions.

Unlike most other occupations, for the attorney, this situation has always been somewhat of a dilemma because the Code of Professional Responsibility for litigators specifically states that they must champion even unpopular causes with zeal once having undertaken a cause. I was somewhat surprised to see that there were more true answers than false. I originally hypothesized that false answers would take nine tenths of the statement. I personally attribute the result to the fact that most litigators in our group have been around past the 10 year learning curve and are now more able to be in a position to pick and choose cases. Unlike the new associate in a firm or a new solo practitioner who must work even unappealing cases to put bread on the table, this response says to me that morally questionable cases are situations where economy normally outweighs integrity and our litigators are simply making a better business decision by taking only better files. Many high profile attorneys take cases just for the notoriety and not the money. Some go broke, others get hired by stars.

Of course we all know about the high profile attorney that we see on television or read about in the newspapers. A distinction must be made here for both high and low Machs with special skills. Both would approach a "game or trial" situation cognitively and play by the specific game rules and definitions. This distinction is based on personality and situational differences and is really not due to any great perception of breaking any social codes. Therefore, I believe that even though there was a close count between those who answered true and false, that for this statement, where special skills and rules apply for attorneys, and given the ambiguous condition at hand, our group is still displaying a low Mach profile. Where normally high Machs initiate and control structures, in this case where ambiguity between social and professional rules exist, the low Mach can still make a claim to fair play and justice.

Statement number three reads: "Anyone who completely trusts anyone else is asking for trouble." The answers to this statement were almost equally divided. We know that high Machs would not trust others, never mind trust them completely and that low Machs would encounter and even change through contacts with others. Therefore we must look a little beyond the surface for an explanation of the data. I would suggest that one reason almost half answered that they could completely trust others and not invite trouble is that, over time, our litigators have fully developed many professional interactions and after a period of time, trust and respect between and among professionals can become relatively secure. There is almost a sense of community among similar professionals and although complete trust is not appropriate for every situation there can be no doubt that working together provides more positive climates. Therefore, these individuals would be considered low Machs. Additionally, neutrality in conveying a non judgmental and accepting attitude, which is a cornerstone of attorney client relations, promotes interpersonal trust.

For the almost half that answered they could not completely trust anyone without asking for trouble is certainly emphasizing the concept of individualism. Here we must ask whether this attitude is attributable to risk or unintentional feelings and attitudes or is it an intentional attempt to conceal?

While we can all sympathize with the person who was recently "burnt" in opening up under similar circumstances, there may be a certain lack of congruence which prevents elevated levels of trust. For instance, the person who laughs while telling you "this is serious" is not congruent and therefore suspect. Additionally, the litigators answering false may be making a distinction between skill and interaction. Most interpersonal situations involve affect to some degree and therefore the critical question is whether or not affect distracts from trust. In other words, the litigator who will not completely trust someone else may be resistant in order to avoid susceptibility to negative influences. Through their own past experiences which they necessarily must bring to bear on a situational encounter, their predictive feedback based on past observable regularities may justifiably support their disconfirmation of another's trust.

I am concluding that the response to this statement still indicates that our litigators are more prone to be low Machs than high Machs. Part of this profile may seem ambiguous to the reader. For this I apologize in that the test instrument can only measure and/or interpret so much. Yet we must not be blind to the important underlying structures which suggest second and third interpretations. Given the underlying considerations inherit in the majority of the litigators interpersonal interactions, these considerations create a strong probability in favor of a low Mach result. While the face of the paper reveals that preponderantly more answered false and therefore as a group, for this statement, they should be considered high Machs, this truth is a particular rather than a general truth. Any truth is unquestionably open to interpretative power where backed by sufficient ingenuity but my conclusion in favor of the second interpretation, that our respondents are low Machs, is more the product of common sense and comes closer to satisfying conditions analogous to those we face on a daily basis. Therefore, I believe my interpretation is more grounded in practice than theory.

Any good interpretation must consider the total framework, in all its possible interrelationships, to build upon a detailed analysis. That attorneys must take sides indicates polarization that translates to trust on one side of an issue and distrust on the other side.

The fourth statement response reassures me that all attorneys aren't crooks. It reads: "The biggest difference between most criminals and other people is that the criminals are stupid to get caught". Obviously this is a view and not a tactic. Again, special knowledge may have played a part in reaching the resulting overwhelming "false" response. Once again I believe this indicates a low Machiavellian attitude. This question or statement has to do with values and suspicions. High Machs are primarily suspicious people and rate fellow beings as significantly less trustworthy than low Machs. However, low Machs are more accurate when determining whether or not something is true or false than high Machs. Low Machs probe for clues and detect deceptions more readily by attending more to and confronting a particular situation.

The fifth statement reads: "It is hard to get ahead without cutting corners here and there." Overwhelmingly our group scored as low Machs. For high Machs details are irrelevant to winning and have a cool detachment which eliminates dangers of interpersonal involvements which might interfere with task achievement. In general, both high and low Machs feel strongly about the positions they hold. High Machs feel that low Machs are naive and behave unrealistically in the real world. Low Machs, on the other hand, see high Machs as reflecting a deplorable lack of compassion and faith in others and as immoral. Again, I would say that our group is moderate to low on the Machiavellian Scale. I believe the major reason for the results so far is that through the rise of modern science and scientific method the logistic method is most often associated with the legal profession. In the past, absent any great transportation, communication or homogeneous structures, analysis or solutions, the Machiavellian method may have been workable. But since Abraham Lincoln first stated that "you can fool some of the people, some of the time, but you cannot fool all the people, all of the time", it is almost of necessity, the lesser of two evils, that our actions and behaviors are determined by the elements and forces at work beneath the surface. Therefore, isn't it correct to assume that, indeed, Abraham Lincoln walked miles through the snow to bring back library books not so much because he was honest but because he wished to mitigate his damages in case he got caught. Really, isn't this what we've been talking about so far concerning the Machiavellian Scale. It doesn't necessarily mean that our respondents are the perfect social prototypes, just that they are intelligent enough to know that history provides a working hypothesis to find the best solutions. In other words, it is not just enough to understand and solve a problem but it is also critical to the litigators' survival to accurately anticipate and avoid pitfalls in method. This is what constitutes a mature experience of the world and depends, to some degree on pre behavior self criticism.

The sixth and final statement of the Machiavellian Scale reads: "When you ask someone to do something for you, it is best to give the real reasons for wanting it rather than giving reasons which carry more weight". Again, overwhelmingly our respondents answered in the low Mach category with 54 "true" responses.

I cannot say for certain that our present day society is becoming increasingly more Machiavellian because I simply do not possess any data that would suggest that to me. However, when this test was first administered in the late 1970s, the conclusion was that we were becoming more Machiavellian. I would submit that, if in fact we are becoming more Machiavellian, it is not occurring in professional occupations and more appropriately may be limited to business-military or corporate lifestyles. One strong reason for this submission is that the person operating within a corporate setting really depends on the setting, (means of production), for his or her basic livelihood. Therefore, this person really does not have the luxury of singular purpose and independent decisions. In turn, this lack of autonomy may perpetuate a Machiavellian behavioral mode for the purpose of obtaining choice and/or freedom instead of being placed in a position of forced choice situations. In other words, it is the litigators' ability to collaborate with open eyes that separates him or her from having to blindly follow instructions as the corporate person oftentimes needs to do. This allows for appropriate, effective and calculating planning, decisionmaking and adjustment of outcome.

In conclusion, when it comes to being measured on the Machiavellian Scale, litigators need not act in a Machiavellian manner. The largest area of independence for the litigator lies in his judgments. It would appear from our responses that moral resolutions are the consensus represented here. Attitudes, motives and frames of action have a social identity because the litigators' actions are almost inseparable from pro social theories. Litigators are not only agents of social philosophies but are agents in determining and performing even in the opposite function when logically formulating dramatic and new social perspectives. Therefore we must see and understand the relationship between the larger social life and the ongoing drama of the litigators' world as reciprocal. He or she is involved as a dynamic character in engendering and engineering the common good.

5

Conflict-Mode Instrument

This is the final chapter that deals with a testing instrument and focuses on the Thomas-Kilman Conflict Mode Instrument designed by Kenneth W. Thomas and Ralph H. Kilman. This instrument scores respondents into five categories; (1) Competing, (2) Collaborating, (3) Compromising, (4) Avoiding and (5) Accommodating.

As the authors note; "competing" is assertive and uncooperative—an individual pursues their own concerns at the other person's expense. This is a power oriented mode, in which one uses whatever power seems appropriate to win one's own position—one's ability to argue, one's rank, economic sanctions. Competing might mean "standing up for your rights," defending a position that you believe is correct, or simply trying to win.

"Accommodating" is unassertive and cooperative—the opposite of competing. When accommodating, an individual neglects their own concerns to satisfy the concerns of the other person; there is an element of self-sacrifice in this mode. Accommodating might take the form of selfless generosity or charity, obeying another person's order when one would prefer not to, or yielding to another's point of view.

"Avoiding" is unassertive and uncooperative—the individual does not immediately pursue their own concerns or those of the other person. They do not address the conflict. Avoiding might take the form of diplomatically sidestepping an issue until a better time, or simply withdrawing from a threatening situation.

"Collaborating" is both assertive and cooperative—the opposite of avoiding. Collaborating involves an attempt to work with the other person to find some solution that fully satisfies the concerns of both persons. It means digging into an issue to identify the underlying concerns of the two individuals and to find an alternative which meets both sets of concerns. Collaborating between two persons might take the form of exploring a disagreement to learn from each other's insights, concluding to resolve some condition which would otherwise have them competing for resources, or confronting and trying to find a creative solution to an interpersonal problem.

Finally, "compromising" is intermediate in both assertiveness and cooperativeness. The objective is to find some expedient, mutually acceptable solution that partially satisfies both parties. It falls on a middle ground between competing and accommodating. Compromising gives up more than competing but less than accommodating. Likewise, it addresses an issue more directly than avoiding, but doesn't explore it in as much depth as collaborating. Compromising might mean splitting the difference, exchanging concessions, or seeking a quick middle ground position (Thomas 10).

Conflict is any situation in which people perceive that others are interfering with their ability to meet their goals. Conflict may be constructive or destructive. For the most part, when two individuals want different things, conflict resolution, more often than not, creates a situation where both must settle for some of one and some of the other. Most people have preferred ways of dealing with conflict and, really, this was the purpose of our testing litigators from coast to coast.

Lets get right to it then; our conflict mode question and answer profile looks like this:

1.   A.   There are times when I let others take responsibility for solving the problem.
     B.   Rather than negotiate the things on which we disagree, I try to stress those things upon which we both agree.

2.   A.   I try to find a compromise solution.
     B.   I attempt to deal with all of his/her and my concerns.

3.   A.   I am usually firm in pursuing my goals.
     B.   I might try to soothe the other's feelings and preserve our relationship.

4.   A.   I try to find a compromise solution.
     B.   I sometimes sacrifice my own wishes for the wishes of the other person.

5.   A.   I consistently seek the other's help in working out a solution.
     B.   I try to do what is necessary to avoid useless tensions.

6.   A.   I try to avoid creating unpleasantness for myself.
     B.   I try to win my position.

7.   A.   I try to postpone the issue until I have had some time to think it over.
     B.   I give up some points in exchange for others.

8.   A.   I am usually firm in pursuing my goals.
     B.   I attempt to get all concerns and issues immediately out in the open.

9.   A.   I feel that differences are not always worth worrying about.
     B.   I make some effort to get my way.

10. A.   I am firm in pursuing my goals.
     B.   I try to find a compromise solution.

11. A.   I attempt to get all concerns and issues immediately out in the open.
     B.   I might try to soothe the other's feelings and preserve our relationship.

12. A.   I sometimes avoid taking positions which would create controversy.
     B.   I will let the other person have some of his/her positions if he/she lets me have some of mine.

15. A.   I propose a middle ground.
     B.   I press to get my points made.

16. A.   I try not to hurt the other's feelings.
     B.   I try to convince the other person of the merits of my position.

17. A.   I am usually firm in pursuing my goals.
     B.   I try to do what is necessary to avoid useless tensions.

18. A.   If it makes other people happy, I might let them maintain their views.
     B.   I will let other people have some of their positions if they let me have some of mine.

19. A.   I attempt to get all concerns and issues immediately out in the open.
     B.   I try to postpone the issue until I have had some time to think it over.

20. A.   I attempt to immediately work through our differences.
     B.   I try to find a fair combination of gains and losses for both of us.

21.   A.   In approaching negotiations, I try to be considerate of the other person's wishes.
     B.   I always lean toward a direct discussion of the problem.

22.   A.   I try to find a position that is intermediate between his/hers and mine.
     B.   I assert my wishes.

23.   A.   I am very often concerned with satisfying all our wishes.
     B.   There are times when I let others take responsibility for solving the problem.

24.   A.   If the other's position seems very important to him/her, I would try to meet his/her wishes.
     B.   I try to get the other person to settle for a compromise.

25.   A.   I try to show the other person the logic and benefits of my position.
     B.   In approaching initiatives, I try to be concerned of the other person's wishes.

26.   A.   I propose a middle ground.
     B.   I am nearly always concerned with satisfying all our wishes.

27.   A.   I sometimes avoid taking positions that would create controversy.
     B.   If it makes other people happy, I might let them maintain their views.

28.   A.   I am usually firm in pursuing my goals.
     B.   I usually seek the other's help in working out a solution.

29.   A.   I propose a middle ground.
     B.   I feel that differences are not always worth worrying about.

30.   A.   I try not to the other's feelings.
     B.   I always share the problem with the other person so that we can work it **out.**

Conflict Mode Instrument

Competing	Collaborating	Compromising	Avoiding	Accommodating
1.	(A = 25)	(B = 47)		
2.	(B = 53)	(A = 19)		
3.	(A = 28)	(B = 43)		
4.	(A = 45)	(B = 29)		
5.	(A = 20)	(B = 51)		
6.	(B = 30)	(A =41)		
7.	(B = 33)	(A = 38)		
8.	(A = 38)	(B = 34)		
9.	(B = 20)	(A = 52)		
10.	(A =15)	(B = 50)		
11.	(A = 37)	(B = 35)		
12.	(B = 55)	(A = 27)		
13.	(B = 28)	(A = 46)		
14.	(B=45)	(A = 27)		
15.	(B = 45)	(A = 27)		
16.	(B= 47)	(A = 24)		
17.	(A = 28)	(B = 44)		
18.	(B = 39)	(A = 32)		
19.	(A = 39)	(B = 33)		
20.	(A = 30)	(B = 38)		
21.	(B = 34)	(A = 35)		
22.	(B =22)	(A = 46)		
23.	(A = 38)	(B = 32)		
24.	(B = 42)	(A = 29)		
25.	(A = 45)	(B = 26)		
26.	(B = 20)	(A = 50)		

27.	(A = 38)	(B = 31)
28.	(A= 33)	(B = 38)
29.	(A = 33)	(B = 37)
30.	(B = 35)	(A = 37)

Totals: (379)   (371)   (530)   (463)   (395)

For the fourth consecutive time the middle ground seems to be an accurate profile of our litigators. Compromising was the number one choice with avoidance number two, followed by collaborating, accommodating and competing, respectively. I was surprised to see such a high index of avoidance but really believe the non litigator might be shocked to lean that our trial attorneys ranked competing at the bottom of the list. However, the answers appear consistent to the litigator, who must be a zealous advocate within the bounds of the law for the client, but, on the other hand, a lawyer has many cases going at any given point in time, most of which he will compromise. In fact, the litigators' living depends on a great extent to and in the amount of the compromises he or she makes to settle the bulk of their case files. Lawyers are therefore brought into conflict with hourly rates, office overhead, time records, scheduling of personal appearances outside of the office, telephone calls, family life, and, not the least important, the devotion to his or her client.

In the above situation, roles and identities must be taken into account and made part of the other's own being. Lawyers, for the most part have strong egos. In fact, it is due to the strong ego that the attorney is a high achiever, and this is positive. However, when the lawyer sees his/her role as the dominating figure, he/she loses sight of objectivity in problem solving and normally closes off alternatives. Of course, sometimes the expert knowledge that the litigator possesses allows him or her to know when closure of alternatives may be useful.

Just received another message on the "internet" which reads as follows: "part of the reason plaintiff attorneys seem more interesting is probably due in part to the fact that they do not need to "fit in" with the large defense firm culture which promotes conformity in practice and attitudes. Conversely, plaintiff attorneys generally reject such "cultures," as evidenced by the far greater percentage of defections from the defense bar to the plaintiffs bar than vice-versa. Plaintiff attorneys generally seem to be freer spirits who accept and assume risk in practice than the defense bar does—particularly when it comes to trial practice. The defense trots out the tried and through; the plaintiff experiments with greater frequency, which is the luxury of being on offense..."

This message is fairly accurate and could possibly explain why only one out of over three hundred defense attorneys answered my ten minute survey. To do so they may have felt that they would be exposed to some risk in practice, after all, answering my survey is not part of their tried and true daily activities. Furthermore, this internet message is important to shore up exactly why our responses have proven our litigators to be real decent people, the complete opposite of the modern day reputation of attorneys as a whole. Our litigators are not "hired guns" as are criminal attorneys or family law attorneys, in fact just about every other legal field of practice charges a retainer up front before services are rendered. Therefore, unlike all other attorneys who may tend to raise or lower their efforts during litigation, depending on the amount of the agreed retainer, the personal injury attorney must be responsive to community standards, mores and values to be able to appreciate case integrity which ultimately translates into dollars and cents. In other words, the bulk of personal injury work is the handling of bona fide cases where the normal person has access to attorneys who work on a "no recovery—no fee" basis. This means that, for the most part, we can calculate the average fee and/or award to be well below the more newsworthy "runaway" verdict that causes so many skewed complaints about the legal profession.

Now, here is another message from the internet. This message comes to us from a non attorney named Pokey. Pokey served on a jury recently and states: "Pokey no lawyer, but her did serve on jury once, just once. Intersection collision and lawyers claim lots of damage, jury we figure it out to $1500 worth of fender damage. Jury ready to go back and Pokey said, wait, what about the lawyer? Others ask what did Poke mean? I said what about the lawyer, the lawyer fee, I said nice lawyer man probably going to charge 30% lets add a little to make lady more whole. So we added $500 to fender damage. Is this wrong? The judge said something about damages to make the person whole or was it hole?

It is hard to utilize strong interpersonal skills with everyone and the above feedback raises more than just the legal question contained therein. Pokey may be considered a person who is difficult to deal with insofar as influencing her behavior to reach a predicted outcome. Even with the best communication skills a litigator may not be able to resolve all conflict with jurors unless individual perspectives can be understood and considered.

Let's take a look at some of the above questions that were answered by an overwhelming majority of our respondents. Question number two proposes a choice between (A) I try to find a compromise situation, and (B) I attempt to deal with all of his/her and my concerns. 53 respondents chose A which is the collaborating or problem solving response and 19 chose B which is a compromising response. In fact, if you scroll through the answer template you will find that the answers which lean heavily for one response are generally found in the compromising or sharing category.

To best interpret the above responses we will use the Thomas-Kilmann guide. Competing responses scored second to last. Those who score highest on the competing profile are the types who are usually surrounded by "yes" men and because they are usually aggressive others tend not to disagree with them which in turn closes off information to the competing type person. Those who score low in this category feel powerless and have trouble taking a firm stand.

The second category of collaboration or problem solving was surprisingly the lowest scoring category. A high score would indicate that our litigators take much time and energy discussing issues in depth even where they do not seem to deserve it. Our litigators scored low which indicates that they do not frequently view differences as opportunities for joint gain. Actually, this is not very surprising given the adverse nature of the business and the fact that the normal relationship between plaintiff and defense counsel does not usually produce mutual gains and/or satisfaction. Furthermore, for the most part it would be unwise to collaborate with an opposing counsel.

Our third category is compromising or sharing which scored highest on our scale indicating a heavy reliance on the practicality and tactics of targeting and trading on the merits of the issues. If our litigators had scored low, this would have indicated that they are too sensitive or embarrassed to be effective in bargaining situations.

Category four which is avoiding or withdrawal scored the second highest rating indicating an abundance of caution and a delay in resolving issues. It can also indicate that others have problems getting their input to the litigator. This really is not entirely surprising as the zealous advocate finds it necessary to stand their own ground while not buying into opposing theories. If our litigators had scored low it would have indicated that they stir up hostilities, feel harried and overburdened.

Finally, category number five which is the accommodating or smoothing category scored third on the scale. Those who would score high feel that their ideas are not getting the attention they deserve. Those who would score low have trouble building goodwill with others.

All in all our litigators continue to exhibit fine personality traits and seem well suited for their occupational niches.

It has become obvious throughout this work that our litigators are not only the trial lawyers and warriors we see and read about in the media but more importantly they are counselors. In other words they are involved in helping the client decide what he or she wants to do. They must provide adequate information in a climate that promotes freedom of choice. Their skills must include such things as reaction or impression management, reflection, empathy and acceptance or rhetorical sensitivity, understanding, honesty, trust, cooperation and coordination which translates to good compromising or sharing skills where a sense of consequence is of utmost importance.

Although there are many intangibles that determine whether or not a particular attorney will be an outstanding trial attorney, there are three basic attributes that an attorney must possess to be a competent trial attorney: (1) knowledge of the law, (2) ability to prepare, and (3) effective courtroom presentation. Of these, the most important is knowledge of the law. Of course, underlying all of this, the lawyer must first have a client, have an understanding of the client's objectives and have an interest in both the person and the cause.

Next to knowledge of the law, the most important factor is the ability to prepare. To that end the litigator must acquire facts from the client to ascertain the nature of the case and as we have stated, sometimes feelings are facts to the client.

What this work has shown is that in addition to knowledge of the law, preparation of the case and courtroom presentation, the successful trial attorney employs common sense.

In conclusion, our litigators get along pretty well with others. We can discern that most of their relationships either work or are amenable to resolution. Our litigators seem to use the most effective behaviors and interpersonal relations because they appear to provide leadership while supporting the client's sense of worth and self esteem. Most importantly they remain focused on their final goal. Our litigators provide power, guidance, security and knowledge and do it in such a way as to be a supplier and not an employer. As our group, on the whole, is over the ten year learning curve, they have personally developed their professional lives so that they increasingly share feelings of recognition and a desire for mutual benefit. Our group seems to have gone beyond the "me first" mentality and, through experience have transformed into high resolution and high influence people.

Summary and Conclusions

Our litigators see the attorney client relationship as that of an agent with professional skills, who acts at all times as a fiduciary with respect to his principal, the client. The attorney sees himself in a somewhat superior position because he or she understands the system within which the parties must operate and because he or she brings an abundance of experience by having gone through many similar situations. However, for the most part, our respondents seem to view the attorney and client in a pretty equal position. The attorney has the edge of vision and insight but the attorney also tries to put the client in the drivers seat with respect to settling or trial decisions.

Interpersonal communications are important in the attorney-client relationship and it seems clear that feedback is necessary for equilibrium. Latitude for improvisation allows for bargaining and interacting in ways possible that lead to higher results.

It is obvious that this statistical analysis is far from technically valid and that its structure leaves much to be desired. However, even with all of its shortcomings, due mostly to lack of resources, participation and overall scope, it still provides plausible answers to modern day hypothetical perceptions and stereotypes. What is valid is that this work provides a more accurate view of the litigator in general and permits insight into how the litigators themselves read situations, interact with others, view themselves and how they undertake task achievement. Although the study was not tightly structured or administered I do not hesitate to make flat, overall comparisons because such interpretations are not entirely accidental or unclassified. For the most part these somewhat unexpected findings were based on a national sample. Contrary to our predictions it appears that litigators are honest, hard working and skillful people. The study did tend to show patterns of responses to tactics, beliefs and attitudes. Additionally, as the models presented, there seems to be a congruence of social balance and moral obligation towards duty.

Let us go back to the beginning questions that were hypothesized concerning the litigators in our survey. The eight, question/statements are as follows:

1. All lawyers care about is winning.

2. All lawyers care about is money.

3. All lawyers care about is power.

4. All lawyers are basically immoral.

5. Lawyers will do anything for money.

6. All lawyers will lie to win.

7. All lawyers are sue happy; and

8. All lawyers are egotistical and self-centered.

We can see that what was hypothesized and what was realized are at different ends of the spectrum. Lawyers care about winning but not to the exclusion of many human factors associated with the litigation process. Lawyers care about more than money even though money is a motivator, they are not blind to courteous ways to achieve it. Power actually rated low for our litigators as the results indicated that higher achievement comes from using techniques other than force of character or position. On our Machiavellian and Rhetorical scales our litigators proved to be very moral. Additionally, lawyers will not do anything for money as most indicated that they will only undertake a cause they believe in. Lawyers also will not lie to win as we saw that our respondents would rather give true reasons to effect change over reasons that might appear to be carry more weight. Our lawyers also do not come across as sue happy, choosing instead to make calculated decisions to undertake litigation. Finally, although lawyers, like all high achievers may have strong egos, their answers indicated that they are far from being self centered individuals, choosing to favor compromise over winner take all or me first attitudes.

Yet why are there those who would still decry that we live in a "culture of warrior litigators." While I agree that we are a litigious society, the system must give access to all those who choose to use it. By precluding people or causes from the system we would silence the very voices that, in the past, have illustrated societal atrocities. What some may consider to be frivolous, others perceive as vital.

Proposed tort reform should not preclude any type of claim. The better approach may be to have claims pre-qualified, with benefit of appeal, but not to just summarily disallow.

We also hear of many attorneys who are dissatisfied with their chosen profession and are making transitions to other career choices. Most lawyers, unlike the public perception, are not rich, must work long hours, sacrifice a stable home environment and have fewer occupational benefits than other occupations. For those few who do make the change, they will still, however, continue to use the skills they developed in practice. Law provides excellent training for analytical thinking and oral and written communication and persuasiveness. Therefore, lawyers are also well suited for careers in business, politics, real estate, banking, finance and communication fields.

In sum, the legal profession has suffered from the media portrayals. Television shows and movies like "L.A. Law" have portrayed the attorney as unethical, dishonest and overly aggressive. Many clients have therefore come to expect their lawyers to act like the attorneys on television. They want their lawyers to try to intimidate the judges, engage in questionable procedural maneuvers and mislead opposing counsel. At the same time clients have become more knowledgeable about lawyering. Most adults have or will be involved in a lawsuit in their lifetime, many average three lawsuits. Therefore, for these "professional plaintiffs", getting more involved in trying to direct legal matters is not uncommon.

Hence, the concept of professionalism is easy to grasp but difficult to measure. Only the lawyers themselves can continue to operate the business of law along the lines of a true profession.

Integrity is the word for this work. It may mean different things to different people, but it certainly means keeping promises, choosing to be accountable and to be faithful. Not only can lack of integrity kill the individual but it can also cut down whole groups of a people as well. The larger issue then is what can you do personally to avoid your own failures and preserve the integrity of the bar? For starters, we can keep it simple. Ideas in theory and ideas in practice should be kept the same. Take the way that seems right, only you have to live with yourself and only you can fool yourself, so don't hide and try to be self respecting and conscience free.

The self regulation of action is dependent on experience and affect. How people behave in a situation depends on how they define it and the personal goals they adopt for the situation. Affective responses are also important in the self regulation process. Lawyers show considerable flexibility in their ability to adjust their perceptions and behavioral strategies to the exigencies of a particular situation. Expertise, based on how much experience a person has in a given situation will also determine flexibility.

Attitudes formed from direct experience, that are accessible, and that reflect self interest or values can predict behavior well. Focusing on reasons underlying one's attitudes can reduce attitude behavior inconsistency, although this tendency is also lessened by whether the behavior is an end in its own right or in service of another goal. How behavior is labeled also influences attitude behavior consistency. Actions may be identified at relatively low levels or they may be identified at higher levels. High level behaviors tend to be more dispositionally based but show more flexibility, whereas low level actions show more stability across situations. Finally, individual differences in how people approach a situation, i.e., self monitoring or self consciousness will influence what attitudes will be salient and guide behavior. Nevertheless these results have indicated a strong consensus and shared commitment of litigators trying to understand themselves and those with whom they come into contact with.

As every experienced defense counsel knows, even the best cases are sometimes lost when attorneys or witnesses fail to communicate, or display negative personality traits that diminish their credibility. Most trial attorneys prepare their witnesses well on facts but do not pay enough attention to the important, but all to often forgotten, witness-jury interaction. Attorneys must be concerned with how the jurors will react to self and to the witness. Conversely, the good plaintiffs attorney is a skilled cross-examiner and will use every trick in the book to make an opposing witness look uncredible. Since jurors are not experts they base their opinions entirely upon their perceptions. Trial lawyers must remember that messages they send to a jury is much more than what is said. It also includes everything jurors hear and perceive about them both cognitively and unconsciously, including attitude, mannerisms, tone of voice, testimony and dress. Character trait projection refers to the primary trait or personality characteristic that attorneys must project to complement, enhance and reinforce the attorneys' case. For example, you may wish to project that you are being alert, trustworthy, savvy or detailed oriented. It is important to keep in mind that jurors view trials as storytelling and drama. All of the litigants and attorneys play certain roles and parts in the story and must be prepared to be evaluated with these roles and parts in mind. In an ideal world, the good guys always prevail and truth needs no window dressing. Unfortunately, in the real world, image often replaces substance and is frequently more persuasive to jurors than integrity alone.

I just received another "net" message which reads "I believe that personality differences lend themselves to quite a few dynamics. For example, plaintiffs' side tends to tell the story better, they are better storytellers and are willing to use presentation technology integrated into their storytelling. They are into empowering the jury. The defense, since it typically represents the corporation or the "big gun" needs to work the liability aspect and has a tougher story to tell".

What we do know is that plaintiffs' attorneys are tolerant. What we don't know is how detailed oriented they are. What we do know is that plaintiffs' attorneys work under less supervision and therefore vary a lot in thoroughness and preparation. What we don't know is if defense attorneys are over supervised by both claims adjusters and partners. What we do know is that plaintiffs' attorneys tend to be expansive in their view of human nature and to focus more on the forest and less on the trees. What we don't know is if defense attorneys are less emotionally involved with their cases. What we do know is that plaintiffs' attorneys are more likely to experience ethical conflict since their income tends to fluctuate more than defense attorneys and they have to pay their own costs. What we don't know is if defense attorneys are more likely to be bored with their careers. What we do know is that plaintiffs' attorneys tend to be more heavily involved and identify with their clients suffering. What we don't know is why defense attorneys are more conservative in dress, speech and manner.

Finally, we know that, according to our national survey and contrary to our predictions, litigators are not alligators in sheep's clothing.

Final Words

Recent rulings to keep cameras out of the courtroom after the O.J. Simpson trial are not in the best interests of our society. The Menendez trial comes to mind. Before I speak more on the current status of cameras in the courtroom, let's explore some legal background.

Historically, only open and obvious abuses of legal proceedings would gravitate to the Supreme Court for a popular ruling. Things like confessions being beaten out of suspects was commonplace before the Miranda decision. We are a society of laws and not of men. Our law is whatever the people say it is. Cameras show true issues and real people and how the court system operates or should operate. Presently, many things go on in a courtroom that have more to do with personalities than with following the rule of law. I personally believe that the riots in Los Angeles could have been avoided after the police were acquitted in the Rodney King trial if society could have kept abreast of the proceedings. Additionally, the Menendez case concerns a grave social issue, child abuse. Furthermore, given that the reasons for a society to punish a wrongdoer are; (1) to deter future similar conduct, (2) to restrain the presently dangerous person, (3) to rehabilitate and (4) to seek retribution; in the Menendez trial, we as a society must determine whether, (1) they must be punished for deterrence reasons, in other words, will they go out and do it again. Unlikely! Because they had only one set of parents. Secondly, should they be punished because they provide a present danger to society. Doubt it! They are not criminal by nature and have no criminal past, nor did they commit the kind of crime likely to be repeated such as robbery, rape, etc.. Third, do they need rehabilitation for the kind of crime they committed. I don't believe most of us have a problem with the concept that if someone is beating you that eventually you will react. Finally, should they be punished for retribution sake, in other words, an eye for an eye. While we all know that what they did was unacceptable given that there were other acceptable alternatives, these are the kind of issues that we should be privy too.

Currently, the office of the District Attorney is a machine and sometimes it is a political machine. In an environment where judges are elected, the District Attorney machine will sometimes take advantage of this to get their way. Other distinctions are more subtle and can take the form of a court ruling that is not entirely appropriate. To my way of thinking, the court proceeding on film, if it influences a difference in behavior, will be for the better because people being watched will act appropriate. For a trial judge to exclude cameras because he or she may act or rule differently is scary because he or she should be constantly fair. Additionally, cameras in the courtroom should promote decorum and propriety among and between the parties, lawyers and jury.

Presently there is a concerted effort to regulate contingency fees. In lawsuits over personal injuries. Lawyers customarily charge a contingency fee *of 25%* to 50% of the award or verdict. This means the lawyer is paid if the case is won and gets nothing if it's lost. This approach is time tested and makes sense. An injured person can get a lawyer's services without paying for them unless there is a successful result. Many people who cannot afford to pay a lawyer's hourly rates can have their cases presented in court. Proponents who would reduce the percentage a lawyer could charge will only hurt the bulk of present day litigants by precluding representation for the common personal injury plaintiff. Lawyers who win or favorably settle a contingency fee case rarely gets paid any more than the time spent on the case justifies. Although we hear of personal injury attorneys earning hundreds of times more with contingency fees than they would if they charged by the hour, it is the rare case indeed where 21 children are killed in a school bus accident. Of course for the bus load of children killed kind of case an attorney would need to be a nincompoop not to get millions of dollars for the clients and hundreds of thousands of dollars in fees. However, the common personal injury case normally settles just short of trial and the average fee generated from a case file is approximately $2000 to $3000. To settle a case after arbitration but before trial normally takes 40 hours and generates enough paper, (of expert legal work), to give the file about 4 inches of thickness. These fees taken by the personal injury litigator are justified and balance out cases where there is not only no recovery but also those cases where the litigator can lose up to $20,000. Where would the common person have access to a system that takes up to $20,000 just to even the odds and risks of litigation. By limiting contingency fees it would logically follow that access by injured persons to lawyers would also be limited. If contingency fees are reduced lawyers may only accept cases if a favorable outcome is reasonably certain based on the facts and the law; the damages suffered by the client will generate enough fees to make taking the case well worth the lawyer's time and only if the defendant is adequately covered by insurance. Reducing contingency fees may cause more harm to society and injured victims than its intended effect which is to keep lawyers from undeserved profits which, as I have already pointed out, is a perception not based in fact.

There are those who advocate letting the common person have access to the courts, change the court system to make it user friendly and put an end to laws written in legalese. However, these advocates have been around for a long time, have published many self help books and yet society, as a whole, still is without access. No ideas generated by these advocates will be successful as long as the common person is still holding down a full time job. Additionally, these ideas will not work for the person on government assistance. There simply is no motivation for the common individual to learn the business of law and therefore the average person needs and will continue to need those people who know the business of law. Similarly, those who advocate a decision making forum outside of the court system where the average person can settle a dispute or claim are kidding themselves if they believe such a forum will make litigants satisfied with the results. Losers will still want to appeal their loss and winners will still want more; such is life! At least the court provides closure and a sense of concreteness that is publicly perceived and therefore it works.

Additionally, there are those proponents who advocate putting an end to punitive damages. In a personal injury case, the jury must decide whether the person being sued caused the victims injuries. If the defendant is found liable, the next question is how much money should the jury award to compensate the victim. If the jury finds that the harm was caused by malicious or intentional conduct, it can punish the defendant based upon the wealth of the defendant. The purpose is to teach the wrongdoer a lesson in a way that makes a strong impact so that the harmful conduct is not repeated. Therefore, punitive damages are essential in evening the odds between the average citizen and the wealthy wrongdoer. Without punitive damages, the wealthy wrongdoer will pay, what to him, is a nuisance verdict and still maintain harmful conduct that normally is the basis of the wrongdoer's wealth. Naturally, just as in every other aspect of life, there are always a few bad apples in every bunch. Proponents seize what appears to be an awkward award and compare it to every case. A recent case in point is the million dollar verdict against McDonald's. What most of society did not hear is that this kind of injury, (caused by hot coffee), had happened on many prior occasions, McDonald's had knowledge of causing prior harm, had knowledge their coffee could cause severe burns in seconds and the amount of the verdict against them represented only one days worth of coffee sales. Has McDonald's changed the temperature of their coffee, and would McDonald's have changed the temperature of their coffee but for punitive damages? Obviously they have, but they would not have without being stung.

Those who advocate an end to punitive damages argue that such damages slows down the introduction of new products. I would argue that we don't need products that would result in punitive damages awards. It is essential to understand that the people who render such awards are average citizens receiving $15 a day for jury duty and, believe me, would not give away ice in the winter time without just cause. The bottom line is that most juries are darn "cheap" when it comes to awarding money. You had better believe that they are not going to reward someone frivolously while they themselves are struggling through life. Those who do receive what the general public would consider to be a "runaway verdict" are those who usually can't use their arms or legs for the rest of their lives.

Lawyers themselves are often perceived as the problem with the legal system and, from time to time, there are those who wish to do away with lawyers altogether. Lawyers are the ones perceived to be taking all the spoils and always end up with a piece of someone's pie. This alone is not the problem, the real problem is the perception of "how" the lawyer goes about dividing up property. They have been portrayed as "sharks", "butchers" and "shysters". Presently, lawyer jokes are in. Some jokes include, "when there are too many lawyers, there can be no justice", "a lawyer is a mouth with a life support system", and "if the laws could speak for themselves, they would complain of lawyers". Yet our survey has indicated otherwise. So, even assuming arguendo that the above is true, it would appear that our respondents realize that they can get more with honey than with vinegar. This kind of approach, (the shark approach), cannot take place unless the personality trait is part of the person. This not being the case, obviously contemporary perceptions of litigators are inaccurate.

The most apparent reason for attacks on attorneys is envy. Envy that non lawyers don't know the jargon, how to find legal information, don't possess an understanding of fundamental legal concepts, how laws link together or are without knowledge of how the system works. We all feel the same way when we go to the garage mechanic. The reputation of businesses in areas of specialization will always be ridiculed. Things lawyers can do that most litigants cannot do by themselves include arguing in court, estimating the odds in court, do competent legal research and probably most important, can get information from other lawyers. Additionally, lawyers can remain rational and objective with a client's case. This fact is so important that it underlies the reason why even lawyers have lawyers for their own claims.

Law, like life in general, contains endless possible troubles. In life we learn that some of the possibilities just aren't all that important. Most of us will never know everything there is to know about a situation but, at least when you have a lawyer for a legal matter, you get to take your best shot.

People will always stereotype attorneys. I don't believe that the contents of this book will change the way attorneys are viewed. This book is just a start to show some true personality traits of the litigator. The litigator is not overly concerned with power, likes their status but do not see themselves as the center of attention, are not control freaks, like to win cases and make money, want respect for their ability but most importantly, treat others with respect and a sense of decency.

My one and only recommendation that I would make based on this study is that future similar studies take place with greater scope and with a more controlled manner. Based on the number of returns I received I would recommend that future surveys become a part of each state's bar exam. All surveys would need to be completed anonymously with no names or numbers provided. Additionally, although many attorneys can rightfully claim privacy rights, a voluntary completion of surveys can be achieved by providing a survey form with bar dues notices that are regularly sent to practicing attorneys. The cost for design and completion can be budgeted from dues. Although most state bars always claim their is not enough money to educate the public and/or provide expanded service to all sectors of society, such studies can go a long way to serve the public interest. Understanding one another can eliminate intimidation and create a more favorable climate. How we choose to deal with one another can and should be constantly improved. Because we choose how to behave, we do more than respond mindlessly to stimuli, we help create the reality that shapes our relationships. Our future choices are limited by the nature of our relationship to the other person and the intensity of another's desire or need to maintain the relationship.

Future surveys in this area can provide greater insight into the complexity of communication. Explanation of concepts, together with a relevant realistic depiction of these concepts in action will help society and the legal profession to improve their interpersonal understandings. An appreciation of the kind of communication and modes of communication in legal reasoning can only improve professional relationships. Feedback, perceptions and blending through an understanding of approaches can confirm both the attorney and client self concept. Future publication of survey results can offer new understandings of how we use language to guide effectively, how to understand the benefits and risks of assertive, non-assertive and aggressive behaviors as these behaviors pertain to attorney-client relationships.

Future studies may also wish to show how style relates to content and conflict resolution. Additionally, future studies should consider the significance of gender and culture to differences in approach to both verbal and nonverbal communication. By getting the public to know who and what attorneys are really made of, trust is advanced. Presently, and obviously, the results of this survey indicate a low level of awareness by the general public because they are not conscious of the litigator's true image.

Another positive possible result of future work in this area is helping attorneys get in touch with themselves, held them clarify their self concept and help them become aware of what contributed to the formation of their self concept. Also, our future choices may be better tuned to reality. We can create reality that is more widely accepted and based on fact rather than myth. When we interact with each other, the influence is mutual and simultaneous. Therefore, true understanding of the litigator will preclude stereotyped misunderstandings and allow for more appropriate feedback.

Lawyers are a culture unto themselves and for the non lawyer to understand our culture we should earnestly attempt to provide the kinds of information to the general public so that they can see things "our way". Before letting society evaluate our culture we would do well to discover for ourselves what the conclusions and norms of our attorney culture are. People interpret their own behavior and the behavior of others on the basis of their cultural norms. To say that others interpretations are wrong is not helpful. To say that these interpretations can lead to misunderstanding is obviously true. The best approach to avoid such misunderstandings is for members of a culture group to become aware that they do not have the same standards for behavior, and then for them to consider in what ways they can change their own behaviors to avoid misunderstanding. Tolerance of the litigation culture is presently low due to ambiguity. Just because the litigation culture is perceived as being separated from society as a whole, it is not without lots of personal identities. Through future studies the thing known as reality of interpersonal interaction will relate an experience to explain what we mean. Not all will change attitudes concerning the legal culture but we can begin to work together to eliminate the stereotypes that strain relationships and limit possibilities. We must develop a proper perspective on our own function in society that goes beyond the conventional wisdom and stereotypes.

Such surveys can also be the work of mandatory continuing legal education. Most importantly, we must put into action what we evaluate to be proper personality traits for the modern day litigator. If we are willing, to gather information that will help solve circumstances then we can influence what approaches are appropriate to eliminate conflict and enhance cooperation in all dealings associated with the legal system.

I leave you with a maxim of the common law; "Equity looks upon that as done which ought to have been done."

Bibliography

Hart, Roderick P., Carlson, Robert E. and Eadie, William F.. "Attitudes Toward Communication and the Assessment of Rhetorical Sensitivity":

Communication Monographs; 47 March 1980.

Lippa, R.. "Expressive Control and the Leakage of Dispositional Introversion—Extroversion During Rote—Playing Teaching" Journal of Personality; 44 1976.

Mader, Thomas F. and Diane C.. "Understanding One Another, Communicating Interpersonally", Brown & Benchmark Publishers, 1993.

Snyder, Mark. "The Many Me's of the Self Monitor". Psychology Today; 13 March 1980.

Thomas, Kenneth W. and Kilman, Ralph KL "Thomas-Kilman Conflict Mode Instrument": Xicom, 1974.

About the Author

Dr. Ryan was born and raised in Pittsfield, Massachusetts and now practices Personal Injury Law in Sacramento, California. He has attended and graduated from Taconic High School in Pittsfield, Massachusetts; Cape Cod Community College in Hyannis, Massachusetts, (A.A.); The American University of Washington, D.C., (B.A., Poli Sci); Troy State University at Hickam Air Force Base, Hawaii extension campus, (M.S., Ed.), University of Honolulu Law School, (J.D.), and LaSalle University, (Ph.D., Ed.).

978-0-595-35534-1
0-595-35534-X

www.ingramcontent.com/pod-product-compliance
Lightning Source LLC
Chambersburg PA
CBHW021004180526
45163CB00005B/1884